All the years at Brooklands

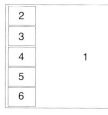

Front cover photographs

1	see page	220
2	see page	2
3	see page	18
4	see page	98
5	see page	110
6	see page	236

The start of a race from the Fork in 1909. The unidentified riders head for the awe-inspiring Members' Banking, with spectators riskily encroaching onto the track.

All the years at Brooklands

Gerry Belton

Centennial Publications

First published June 2007 by Centennial Publications,
Wiveliscombe, Somerset TA4 2TA

Copyright © Gerard Belton

A CIP catalogue record of this book
Is available from The British Library

ISBN   978 – 0 – 9546798 – 2 - 8

Typesetting, page design and layout by Artwork Marketing

Printed in England by the Cromwell Press, Trowbridge, Wiltshire

H Le Vack 245cc New Imperial-JAP	136	
J S Wright 344cc Zenith-JAP	138	
C S Staniland 490cc Norton	140	
C Temple 996cc Montgomery-British Anzani	142	
A Denly 490cc Norton	144	
The Pond Start Public Enclosure	146	
C W G Lacey 344cc Cotton-JAP	148	
T R Allchin 996cc Zenith-JAP	150	
R M N Spring 490cc Norton	152	
R E Humphries 989cc Harley-Davidson s'car	154	
R T Grogan 490cc Norton	156	
The Brighton Speed Trials	158	

1925	**H M Walters** 344cc Jappic	160
	J Emerson 994cc Zenith-Blackburne	162
	J W Wheeler 494cc Douglas	164
	J S Wright 980cc Zenith-JAP	166
	R Kaye Don 344cc Zenith-JAP	168
	P G Dallison 170cc Elfson-Norton	170

1926	**G C Cobbold** 493cc Sunbeam	172
	G L Wallis 344cc Wallis-JAP	174
	A F Hamilton 348cc Velocette	176
	V E Horsman 599cc Triumph s'car	178
	C W G Lacey 344cc Grindlay Peerless-JAP	180

1927	**J S Wright** 996cc Brough Superior-JAP	182
	H G Grose 347cc Matchless	184
	C W G Lacey 488cc Grindlay Peerless-JAP	186
	A Denly 490cc Douglas	188
	J S Worters 246cc Excelsior-JAP	190
	C S Staniland 344cc Excelsior-JAP	192
	P Brewster 996cc Zenith-JAP s'car	194
	R N Judd 494cc Douglas	196
	F W Dixon 996cc Brough Superior-JAP	198

1928	**H Le Vack** 496cc New Hudson	200
	C W G Lacey 499cc Grindlay Peerless-JAP	202
	E C E Baragwanath Brough Superior-JAP s'car	204

1929	**C J Williams** 495cc Raleigh	206
	J S Wright 996cc Zenith-JAP	208
	G H Tucker 588cc Norton s'car	210
	J S Wright 996 Zenith-JAP	212
	A Denly 346cc AJS	214
	G E Nott 499cc Rudge Whitworth	216

1930	**C S Staniland** 248cc Rex-Acme-Blackburne	218

1931	**O M Baldwin** 980cc Zenith-JAP	220
	C B Bickell 497cc Bickell-JAP	222
	E C E Baragwanath Brough Superior-JAP s'car	224
	A L Loweth 497cc Loweth-JAP	226

1932	**The 100 Miles Junior Grand Prix Race**	228
	The 100 Miles Senior Grand Prix Race	230
	The Hutchinson Hundred Day Handicap Race	232

1933	**M B Saunders** 246cc Excelsior-JAP	234

1934	**S. Wood** 492cc New Imperial	236
	Hutchinson Hundred Day	238
	Miss Beatrice Shilling 490cc Norton	242
	E C Fernihough 172cc Excelsior-JAP	244

1935	**C K Mortimer** 490cc Norton	246
	C B Bickell 499cc Ariel s'car	248
	H R Nash 123cc New Imperial	250

1936	**BMCRC Cup Day Meeting**	252

1937	**Senior Brooklands Road Championship Race**	254

1938	**E C Fernihough** 996cc Brough Superior-JAP	256
	E C Fernihough 996cc Brough Superior-JAP	258
	D A Loveday 497cc Triumph	260
	A C Perryman 248cc Excelsior	262

1939	**I B Wicksteed** 496cc Triumph	264
	N Pope 996cc Brough Superior-JAP	266
	BMCRC Mountain Championship Day	268

Herbert Le Vack 1887 – 1931	270

Preface

On 10 April 1920 my father, Joseph Bayley, saw his first motorcycle race meeting at Brooklands, the first proper meeting there after the 1914-18 war.

Aged 13 and completely smitten, he went to five more that year. School and illness made visits less frequent for the next two years but he cannot have missed many motorcycle races at the track between 1923 and 1933, getting to know most of the riders, tuners and owners well.

His passion was very fast machines on the outer circuit, explaining in part his less frequent visits when 'road' racing on the slow mountain circuit increased in prominence. The meeting of 15 July 1939 was his last prior to the track's closure by war.

In 1923 my father began to gather his photographic record of races and riders at Brooklands, initially by assisting a circuit photographer, and subsequently by using this expert's equipment. Sadly, his prints were destroyed in the London blitz. Years later, with the acknowledged help of Harry Louis, the editor of 'The Motor Cycle', his collection was expanded to over 330 photographs. Of these, 130 appeared in his 1968 book, "The Vintage Years at Brooklands". Many of the remainder, together with his notes on them, feature in this book.

Joseph Bayley was not merely a knowledgeable observer of racing at Brooklands. In 1928, he acquired a V-twin Croft Cameron Anzani previously raced there. He used it mainly for rapid trips between London and Devon. In 1929, with tuner Lawrence Hartley's help, a pair of Ariel cylinder barrels and heads were fitted, having both exhaust ports forward facing to help cooling. A genuine engineering 'first', impressing even Eric Fernihough. To his stable he added Knight's Zenith-JAP, in its day capable of lapping the track at 110mph, and a Brooklands framed, vintage Douglas.

In 1947 my father took me to Brands Hatch, then a grass track, to meet many of his Brooklands friends, some still competing successfully. Smitten too, my interest in motorcycle racing has never waned.

As a teenager I used to accompany Len Cole to sprint events with my father's very quick Douglas. When Len was involved in forming the National Sprint Association, he asked me to run its timing equipment. Sydney Allard's introduction of American drag racing to England in 1963 found me timing the 190mph cars, getting to know both him and his PRO Gerry Belton, and working with them for two years.

Last year, Gerry suggested republishing "The Vintage Years at Brooklands". However a sequel, envisaged by my late father, seemed a better idea. Gerry has produced a fascinating book, combining factual details with an evocative portrayal of the lives of the motorcycle racing community throughout all the years of Brooklands.

My father would have approved.

Dr Anthony Bayley   Folkestone June 2007

Author's Introduction

Brooklands motor racing circuit was built by a wealthy Surrey landowner on his large country estate close to the pleasant town of Weybridge in wooded heathland typical of that part of the county.

The landowner, H J Locke King, retained engineers and contractors to lay a quarter of a million tonnes of concrete on his property to form an enormous banked oval track, 100 feet wide and 2.7 miles long, on which motor cars could be tested and raced. In the centre would be an airfield, hangers and an aircraft factory or two. No planning permission for this astonishing development was sought. None was needed, for all this was a hundred years ago.

Hugh Locke King's great project was to succeed beyond his expectations, Brooklands effectively becoming the birthplace of the British motor and aviation industries. The circuit was to become hugely popular with the public – if not local residents – with people flocking to car race meetings drawn by the famous Brooklands slogan, 'The right crowd and no crowding', designed to appeal particularly to fashionable society.

Motorcycle race meetings at Brooklands did not generally appear to fit into this category. Apart from the events put on from time to time by the Public Schools and the University clubs, the crowds at most motorcycle race meetings were quite small but made up of enthusiasts. A proportion of the population in those days who could not afford a motor car would own a motorbike or sidecar combination and knowing how they worked would become knowledgeable spectators at the motorcycle meetings as well.

Even in the Brooklands paddock, the 'them and us' tradition persisted. The car racing people used the swish restaurant and bar in the Club House, the bike men and their mates, the tatty cafeteria nearby.

This book, then, is about the latter, most of them clever, sometimes self-taught engineers who tuned and raced their machines at the track, often having to live on a comparative shoestring. The opportunity to tell their story arose when Tony Bayley agreed to my developing an idea that his father Joseph had had for a sequel to his iconic "The Vintage Years at Brooklands". This is the result.

It is not a technical survey of the development of the British motorcycle over four decades. I lack the technical knowledge for such a book. It is simply an attempt based on research and a feeling for social history, to paint a picture of the lives of the men who worked and competed at the track, creating as they did so, a unique atmosphere and tradition which one can still feel at Brooklands even today, nearly seventy years since the last race took place at the track.

In some respects, like Joseph Bayley's volume, this is really a picture book with words. But, even if the words in this case do not satisfy the reader, I believe that a study of the photographs definitely will.

Gerry Belton   Minehead   June 2007

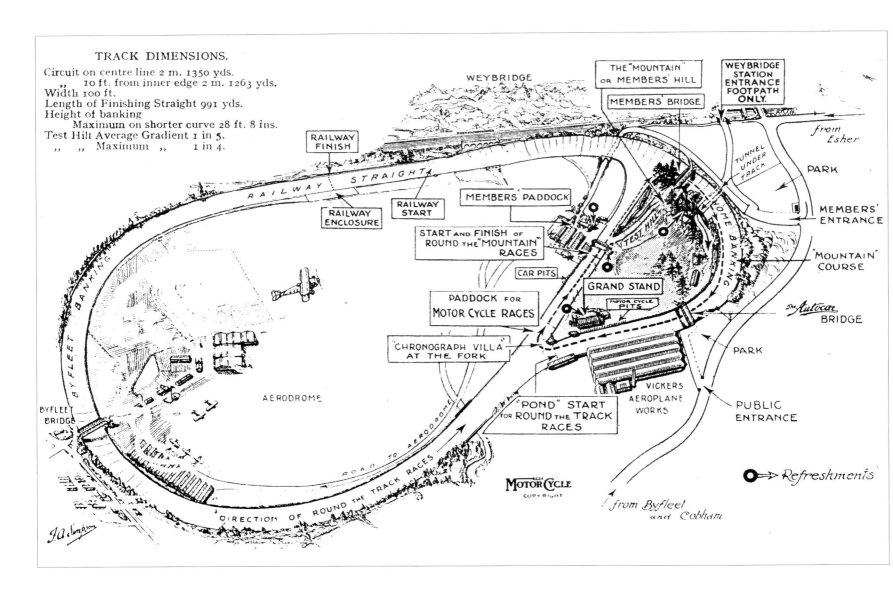

TRACK DIMENSIONS.

Circuit on centre line 2 m. 1350 yds.
    ,,   10 ft. from inner edge 2 m. 1263 yds.
Width 100 ft.
Length of Finishing Straight 991 yds.
Height of banking
    Maximum on shorter curve 28 ft. 8 ins.
Test Hill Average Gradient 1 in 5.
    ,,   ,,   Maximum   ,,   1 in 4.

WEYBRIDGE

THE "MOUNTAIN" OR MEMBERS' HILL

MEMBERS' BRIDGE

WEYBRIDGE STATION ENTRANCE FOOTPATH ONLY.

from Esher

PARK

RAILWAY FINISH

RAILWAY STRAIGHT

RAILWAY ENCLOSURE

RAILWAY START

MEMBERS PADDOCK

TUNNEL UNDER TRACK

MEMBERS' ENTRANCE

START AND FINISH of ROUND the "MOUNTAIN" RACES

TEST HILL

"MOUNTAIN" COURSE

CAR PITS

The Autocar BRIDGE

BYE FLEET BANKING

GRAND STAND

PADDOCK FOR MOTOR CYCLE RACES

MOTOR CYCLE PITS

PARK

"CHRONOGRAPH VILLA AT THE FORK"

AERODROME

"POND" START FOR ROUND THE TRACK RACES

VICKERS AEROPLANE WORKS

PUBLIC ENTRANCE

BYFLEET BRIDGE

ROAD TO AERODROME

Refreshments

THE MOTOR CYCLE
COPYRIGHT

from Byfleet and Cobham

DIRECTION OF ROUND THE TRACK RACES

J.A. Simpson

10

The Brooklands Motor Course

At the beginning of the twentieth century, the British public as a whole regarded the motor car as a noisy, dirty and unreliable contraption of interest only to the very well-to-do. There was neither awareness of, nor interest in the progress being made by foreign motor manufacturers able to test their designs on long and mainly straight roads.

The British motor industry on the other hand was handicapped by the constraints put on design and development by the 20mph speed limit imposed under the Motor Car Act of 1903 and road surfaces only suitable for horse-drawn vehicles.

This was seen with clarity by a wealthy Surrey landowner, H F Locke King, who, with the support of a number of like-minded men of substance, resolved to turn his Brooklands estate in wooded heathland near Weybridge into a huge banked concrete circuit for sustained high speed motor car testing and racing.

Colonel Holden RE was appointed to design the course and oversee the civil engineering. The track would be roughly oval in shape, running south-west to north-east, 100ft wide throughout and 2.7 miles long. To the south was the longer of the two banked curves, the Byfleet Banking, with a 17ft elevation, falling away to cross the River Wey. Then came a reverse curve past what was later to become the Vickers aeroplane works, before climbing to the acute northern banked curve, the Members' Banking, rising to 32ft, with a maximum inclination of 1 in 2.

The two main curves were linked by the Railway Straight, over half a mile long, alongside the main Woking to London railway line. The Finishing Straight left the Outer Circuit at the Fork, running almost due north for nearly 1000 yards, emerging on the Members' Banking near the bridge.

Work started late in 1906 with the excavation of vast amounts of earth, followed by the laying of 250,000 tonnes of concrete in a six inch thick layer over the whole area of the track, including the 'flying' sections of the bankings. The immense task occupied up to 2000 men, 700 of whom are said to have worked day and night throughout the winter.

Colonel Holden's masterpiece was completed in the spring of 1907, the official opening taking place on 17 June. A fortnight later, S F Edge would be first to use the track for record breaking, averaging over 65mph for 24 hours in one of his huge Napier cars, supported by two others. It was later suggested that this pounding on the still uncured concrete was one reason for the future unevenness of the course.

A tunnel under the track gave access to the infield where there was seating for thousands of spectators, mostly on the Members' Hill. Some 13,000 people did turn up for the first car race meeting on 6 July, to find that horse racing tradition had been followed, with drivers wearing their colours and terms such as 'paddock' in use. And, from the first day to the very last, the bookies' blackboards were to be in evidence.

H CISSAC   16hp Peugeot   27 July 1905

Motorcycle racing in Britain in the first years of the twentieth century mainly consisted of sprints, hill climbs and races on cycle tracks, often on board surfaces. The only road racing took place in France and Austria, the rules tending to favour purpose-built lightweight machines with very large engines. British riders who had taken part on the Continent disliked this form of racing, as it negated the development of motorcycles suitable for public roads. A movement established to encourage motorcycle road racing in Britain under the rules of the Auto Cycle Club, later to become the Auto Cycle Union, led to an approach to the Manx Government for a road race in the Isle of Man to be arranged for 1907.

Additionally, construction of the forward-looking 2.7 mile banked circuit on the Brooklands estate in Surrey of landowner H J Locke-King was due to commence in 1906.

Thus would soon be met the aspirations of the skilled and dedicated British motorcycle engineers and riders, especially those having an eye on the speed records so far held by French machines such as the one seen here.

Powered by a huge, 16hp (2500 cc) V-twin Peugeot engine, this 110lb machine was ridden by Frenchman Henry Cissac, ironically on the Blackpool seafront, on 27 July 1905, to a flying-start kilometre record of 87.32mph. Later in the year, the Italian rider J Guippone used the same machine to set up a new one hour record of 63.61mph, this time on the Parc des Princes circuit, near Paris.

In 1907, the opening of the motor course at Brooklands would allow both the nascent British motor car and the so far hesitant motorcycle industries to look forward to the future with justifiable confidence.

W E COOK 7.9hp Peugeot-NLG 20 April 1908

As far as anyone knows for certain, the first motorcycle race to take place on the new Brooklands motor course in Surrey was between two Oxford undergraduates on Tuesday, 25 February 1908, some eight months after the circuit was opened for motor car racing.

   This was a private match race, approved by the track authority, the Brooklands Automobile Racing Club. W Gordon McMinnies had brought his 3.5hp TT Triumph down to take on the 5hp TT Vindec-Special of his friend Oscar Bickford. The equivalent capacity of the two machines was approximately 500cc and 750cc. The winner of the one lap race from a standing, or perhaps running, start was McMinnies, by 150yards, at an average speed of 53.55mph.

   Witnessing the race was the BARC Secretary, Mr E de Rodakowski, who was intrigued enough to invite several prominent motorcyclists to take part in a motorcycle race to be staged during the forthcoming Easter Monday meeting on 20 April.

In the event, as many as twenty-two riders lined up on the day, including the experienced Collier brothers on their fast Matchless machines. Several other marques were also represented on the start line, Triumph, NSU, Rex, Chater-Lea, Minerva, BSA and FN, amongst others.

   The easy winner of the two lap, five and a half mile race was Will Cook on his 7.9hp (1000cc) Peugeot - NLG, built by North London Garages. His speed was 63mph and his winner's purse twenty-five guineas, a quite substantial sum of money in those days.

   In the poor quality but historic photograph across the page, the tall race winner Cook is seen posing with his big unsprung machine, of which he was to say that due to the bumps on the track he was hardly ever in the saddle.

   The semi-circle of admirers in pictures of motor-cycle race winners was to become just one of many Brooklands traditions throughout the years.

Return to the track   3 October 1908

It was reported that everyone present at Brooklands' first motorcycle race, described on the previous page, agreed that the event was a success. The only reservation was that a handicap system such as that already in use for car races would have to be introduced if motorcycle racing was to become a popular feature at the track. This was tried out the following May when thirty riders took part in a race with handicaps based on performances in the previous race.

Meantime, a case brought by local residents against the owner of the track, Mr Locke King, for 'causing noise nuisance' had gone against him and he was fined £7,000. Concerns about noise had first arisen over the twenty-four hour record attempt with Napier cars by S F Edge in June 1907, since when car racing with open exhausts had continued unabated.

Nevertheless, the introduction of motorcycle racing appeared to have been the last straw and the BARC realised that here was a convenient scapegoat. The Club therefore announced that no motorcycles would be permitted on the track until further notice.

Eventually, however, by the autumn of 1908 tempers appeared to have cooled down, and the BARC relented, deciding, to the relief of the motorcycling fraternity, that a two lap motorcycle handicap race would be included in the Club's meeting on 3 October.

Twenty-eight machines were entered. In the picture, riders are seen gathering in the Paddock in preparation for the race. In the background is the new results tower, based on those at horse racecourses. Competitors and their numbers would be displayed, the numbers being indicative of their handicap start, the rider on scratch being number 1. The race on this occasion was won by G Gibson on a 3.5hp Triumph at 53mph.

A G REYNOLDS   6hp Matchless-JAP   25 March 1909

On 25 March 1909, the Brooklands Test Hill was formally opened. This was the brainchild of the BARC's new Clerk of the Course, Major Lindsay Lloyd, who felt that such an innovation would enliven proceedings at the track.

Starting from opposite the paddock, the hill ran, and still does run, for 352 feet up the side of the Members' Hill, with an initial slope of 1 in 8, increasing to 1 in 4 towards the top.

On the day of the opening, George Reynolds, on his single-geared Matchless, was the first motorcyclist to attempt the climb. With a generous run-in and a leap into the saddle, he climbed to the top in 6.17 seconds at an average speed of 38.9mph.

Coincidentally, Reynolds had been one of a number of motorcyclists at Brooklands who disliked having to depend on the occasional invitation from the Brooklands Automobile Club to use their machines on the track.

He had therefore conceived the idea of a separate club, leading to the formation of the British Motor Cycle Racing Club in March 1909, the month of the opening of the Test Hill. Reynolds was to serve either as its honorary secretary or timekeeper during the thirty years history of Brooklands.

With the club's full title proving to be something of a mouthful, BMCRC (or Bemsee, to choice) became the accepted usage, as it is to this day.

R T EXSHAW and F W BARNES   3.5hp Zedette-JAPs   April 1909

Both riders have been testing their machines in preparation for the Brooklands Automobile Racing Club's Easter motor race meeting in April 1909.

On each of the three days there were to be held two races for motorcycles. On Easter Monday, Barnes, on the right, finished third in the two lap Surrey Motor Cycle Handicap Plate.

Two weeks earlier he had established the first standing start record for the newly built Test Hill in a time of 18.63 seconds. In October of the following year, 1910, he improved that to 12.26 seconds, a record that was to stand until 1921.

Designed by Barnes and built at his nearby Zenith Motor Works, the Zedettes were fitted with his patented Gradua variable gear system.

Operated by a handwheel on the side of the petrol tank, this device moved the belt-driven rear wheel forward or backward, expanding or contracting the engine pulley to give gear ratios ranging from three and a half to one to nine to one. This gave the rider considerable advantage at a time when most of the other machines used for racing were single-geared.

Over the ensuing years until right up to the late twenties, many of the leading Brooklands motor-cycle exponents used Zenith machines, with or without the Gradua gear, especially in the bigger engine capacity classes.

As can be seen here, Freddie Barnes believed in campaigning his own products from the very earliest days of racing at the track.

H H BOWEN   3.5hp Trump-JAP   22 April 1909

Harold Bowen made his first appearance at the first meeting run by the newly formed British Motor Cycle Racing Club, on 22 April 1909.

He is seen here, on his 3.5hp Trump-JAP, number 15, leading Gordon McMinnies and J T 'Billy' Bashall, both on similar machines, in the first scratch race run that day over two laps for machines up to 1000cc. Bowen was to finish in third place behind an NSU and an NLG-Peugeot, both of which had 7hp engines.

Shortly after this event Bowen was to turn out on a 964cc BAT-JAP, taking a third place at the 19 May meeting and a second place in two races at the BMCRC third meeting in June.

In July, at the new club's next meeting, Bowen scored again, this time with his smaller 3.5hp BAT-JAP. The three lap race was for novices, defined as riders not having won a race before. The machines also had to actually belong to the rider! Bowen won from a 1 minute 12 second handicap start, at a speed of nearly 63mph, the fastest speed yet for an under 500cc machine.

Then, at the BMCRC members' meeting the following August, in unusually cold and windy conditions, Bowen on his 3.5hp BAT-JAP won the all-comers one hour race.

For the following year, 1910, Bowen had fitted a 658cc JAP engine to his BAT, winning the 750cc class time trial at the 13 April BMCRC meeting. Later in the day, in heavy showers, he won the hotly contested one hour TT race from the Collier brothers on the Matchless Company's TT machines.

Bowen's last outing was at a BARC meeting on 27 April, but plug trouble restricted him to only fourth place in the Weybridge Motor Cycle Handicap, and a rather disappointing end to an otherwise remarkably successful, if short, Brooklands career. Quite possibly, as a young man, he thought that settling down in a more financially secure and safe occupation might be a preferable option.

H A COLLIER 862cc Matchless-JAP 22 April 1909

On the previous page we read about Harold Bowen, who came third in the first of two scratch races at the first ever race meeting of the newly formed BMCRC on 22 April 1909.

Winner of the second of the two races for machines up to 1000cc was Harry Collier, seen here on his 7hp Matchless-JAP. Recognisable from his trademark moustache and heavy spectacles, he is posed on what is probably the Matchless on which at Brooklands, in early May 1909, he covered 775 miles in 24 hours, an average speed of 32.32mph, and a new British motorcycle record.

He is clearly equipped for all eventualities, with spare drive belt, extra oil tank, and tool box. On the other hand, he has the benefit of neither clutch nor gearbox.

Earlier, in 1908, Charlie Collier had covered over 68 miles in one hour on a 964cc V-twin JAP engined TT Matchless, thus breaking the world record previously held by Peugeot.

The Matchless motorcycle had emerged from the steam laundry business of Collier and Sons which had some time before diversified into the manufacture of bicycles. It was the sons, Harry and Charlie, who had influenced the further step into motorcycle production and both were soon demonstrating the potential of their products, firstly in the Isle of Man and now, by winning races and taking records at Brooklands.

Harry, and particularly his brother Charlie were to figure prominently during the early years at Brooklands, riding their big Matchless machines with almost monotonous success.

The Indian Team   638cc Indian V-twins   16 March 1910

Seen here are most of the Indian team present at the BMCRC's first meeting of 1910. This event was remarkable as being the first ever motor-cycle race attended by royalty, in the person of Francis, Prince of Teck, father-in law to the then Prince of Wales.

The team was entered in the one hour race for machines conforming to Tourist Trophy regulations, although on this occasion, the mudguards could be discarded. All the Indian machines were the new ohiv 638cc V-twins, now fitted with mechanical oil pumps, thus doing away with the need to remove a hand from the handlebars to work the pump, just one of many hazardous operations familiar to riders of most early machines at Brooklands.

Those appearing in the picture are, from left to right, J Gibson, A J Moorhouse, C B Taylor, C E Bennett, D R Clarke and W O Bentley. The Indian Company concessionaire in Britain,

'Billy' Wells is standing at the back. Bentley was later to become a name to conjure with in the field of quality motor cars. Arthur Moorhouse, unhappily, was to lose his life in 1912, still riding for Indian, to become one of only two motorcycle racing fatalities in the track's history.

The one hour race on this occasion also broke new ground in that, for the first time, pushers were allowed to help riders start their machines in a race. The large field therefore got away unusually well, but despite the efforts of so many of the other top riders in the race, the new Indians proved to be too strong, the first three places being taken by Bennett, Bentley and Guy Lee Evans. The latter is shown, on his 497cc machine, on page 34.

The Prince of Teck presented the prizes, including a silver cup for the winner, Charlie Bennett, the cup having been put up by Billy Wells himself!

W D CHITTY   270cc Givaudan   13 April 1910

Chitty made his first appearance at Brooklands in the second of the two motorcycle races included in the last BARC meeting of 1909. He rode a 340cc Frays-JAP to win the Autumn Handicap, at a very respectable speed, in those days, of over 50 mph.

Early in 1910, he had come across the little 270cc Givaudan we see here, which qualified for the smallest capacity Class A, up to 275cc. Despite the foreign-sounding name, this was a British-built motorcycle. At that year's BARC Easter Monday meeting, Chitty was able to claim a Class A world's record of 50.50mph over the flying start mile.

For the record time trials in June, he used both machines to good effect, with a new Class A record at 52.05 mph and, more importantly, 61.38mph in Class B, up to 350cc, so becoming the first rider at Brooklands officially to exceed 60mph on a three-fifty.

Later in the summer of 1910, he experimented with a 482cc JAP engine in the Frays, fitted with an unusual twin exhaust port head. However, he was soon back on the Givaudan, improving his own Class A record to 52.67mph.

By September, he appeared to have got the bigger engined Frays-JAP running well enough to win the one hour scratch race for 'The Motor Cycle' journal's challenge cup, up to 500cc, at a speed of 53mph.

For the May meeting of the following year, Chitty had refitted the 340cc JAP engine in the Frays to win a three-lap handicap race at a remarkable speed of 57mph, enough to beat Jack Haswell's 499cc Triumph off the same handicap start.

Later in the year, he had made yet another, and now final change, back to Class A, with a 272cc JAP motor fitted in the Frays; but with no apparent success.

The photograph merits study, even if only to imagine what Brooklands riders had to cope with in the early years. Most machines had no clutch, gears, brakes, or fork suspension and the drive to the rear wheel was by means of a rubber and canvas belt. In this case, Chitty even did without a saddle, remarkable in view of the bumpy track. Finally, engine lubrication was by hand pump, one hand having to be taken off the handlebars at regular intervals, and at full speed.

E C W FITZHERBERT 448cc FN 22 June 1910

Fitzherbert campaigned this smart, road-going Belgian machine during 1910, undoubtedly making best use of the flexible four cylinder in-line engine and shaft drive.

Having come in second to the redoubtable Harry 'Wizard' Martin in the BARC Easter Monday Spring Handicap over five laps, he entered the challenging sixty lap Brooklands TT race arranged for Wednesday, 22 June. Taking place during the fourth BMCRC meeting of 1910, this was to be the first long distance motorcycle race at Brooklands, the sixty laps totalling 164 miles.

One of the purposes of the race was to allow for testing the durability of multi-cylindered machines with particular relevance to the TT.

The race was for just two classes: one for singles up to 500cc, the other for those multis up to 670cc. The race was to start and finish at the Fork where pit arrangements were set up. Only one pit helper per rider was permitted.

The start for the twenty singles and eighteen multis was simultaneous and, once all had got their engines started it would have been a splendid sound. For whilst local residents were again complaining, exhausts were still open.

Because of the length of the race the pits saw frequent visits, not only for fuel and oil, but to rectify such problems as stretched valves, slipping driving belts and tyre failure. There were several retirements, one due to a high speed tumble, happily with just a few bruises to show for it.

In just under three hours, the overall winner turned out to be a multi – A J Moorhouse on a 639cc Indian V-twin, at a speed of 56.72mph. The singles class winner was F A McNab's 488cc Trump-JAP, at 53.71mph.

Into fourth place in the multi-cylinder class rode Fitzherbert on his reliable FN, having disposed of the challenge from the other FN rider in the race, R O Clark. Fitzherbert's average speed for the sixty laps was a decent enough 43.34mph.

FN motorcycles were to feature regularly in races at Brooklands throughout the early years. Particularly, Clark was still campaigning his machines right up to November 1913, when he broke long distance and time records up to 250 miles and six hours. For these records he used a 273cc FN, causing the race press reporter to express surprise in view of 'the rider's handicap of weighing over fourteen stone'.

H MARTIN   344cc Martin-ASL-JAP   24 August 1910

Harry Martin was to become one of the outstanding engineer/riders during the early years at Brooklands. He is first reported as taking part in a race during the BARC's Easter meeting in 1909, riding a JAP-engined machine of his own manufacture.

Having severed earlier connections with the Collier family's Matchless concern, Martin set up on his own at the track, and his machines were soon being taken seriously. At the record time trials in August that year, the 350cc class was won on a Martin-JAP, and again the following October. In March 1910, the designer himself appeared on his latest model, this one powered by an over-square, 85x60mm JAP unit, giving him a handsome win in a BMCRC all-comers' handicap race.

As seen in the picture on the far right, the new Martin was fitted with experimental pneumatic leading-link front forks, specially made for Harry Martin by Air Springs Ltd.

Indefatigable in his search for more power and reliability, Martin continued to amass class wins on his 344cc machines. Here, at the record time trials in August 1910, Martin had excelled himself, taking the flying start kilometre and mile records to 68.28 and 65.97mph respectively,

thereby also exceeding the current 500cc class records. It was widely believed that, by then, Martin was using alcohol as a fuel additive.

The Martin-JAP was not only a successful racing motorcycle but also one having fine lines and showing outstanding attention to detail, as can be seen from the picture below. The frame would take either the 250 or 350cc JAP engines and Martin himself used a 498cc V-twin version to set a new 500cc flying start kilometre record of 73.95mph in August 1911.

GUY LEE EVANS   497cc Indian   5 October 1910

This is one of the Indian machines that Evans raced during 1910. It is chain-driven and has the new overhead inlet valve, single-cylinder engine.

He is seen here during the last BARC meeting of 1910, having come second to Harry Martin's 344cc Martin-ASL-JAP in a new-style handicap race for all classes of machines not having previously lapped in excess of 60mph. The race distance was five and a half miles, and it had started at the Fork.

For the second race of the day, Evans switched to one of the Indian team's big 994cc twin-cylinder machines and won in a new Brooklands three lap motorcycle race speed record of 73.75mph. Second and third places went to Charlie and Harry Collier on their 976cc Matchless-JAP machines.

The American-built Indians had made their first appearance at Brooklands at the BMCRC meeting of Wednesday, 10 May 1909. They were ridden by the American, W H 'Billy' Wells, Indian's agent in Britain, and the ex-Rex rider, Guy Lee Evans. In a two lap handicap race for motorcycles up to 1000cc, Evans came second on a 2.5hp (350cc) model whilst Wells finished in fourth place in his 5hp (750cc) machine.

Subsequently, Evans rode exclusively for Wells with considerable success and took several more Brooklands distance records on the 497cc single- cylinder Indian seen here.

C R COLLIER   998cc Matchless-JAP   15 July 1911

Charlie Collier is pictured, on the right, ready for his series of match races with the American Jake de Rosier on his Indian, on Saturday 15 June 1911. Collier's 998cc Matchless-JAP is fitted with a single Amac carburettor. He had also added a Union Jack flag for the occasion.

Of the two Collier brothers, Charlie was undoubtedly the outstanding promoter on the track of the family's Matchless factory products. Both men had cut their teeth on the board tracks, including that at Canning Town, London, which were the only places in the UK, where, hitherto, motorcycle racing could take place.

So the opening of the new Brooklands track in 1907 had been greeted with enthusiasm by the whole of the British motorcycle racing fraternity, the Matchless team in particular. After a trial outing in 1908, in an invitation motorcycle race during the BARC's first ever Easter Monday meeting, Charlie Collier began to make plans for an attempt on the world's one hour record, standing since 1905 to J Giuppone, on a 16hp (2500cc) Peugeot at 63.61mph.

Collier made his attempt on the record on 8 October 1908, riding a 964cc TT Matchless-JAP, belt driven, with no clutch, gears or throttle. His standing lap was already at record speed and he kept going so well that, when the hour

was up, he had become the new world's record holder at 68 miles and 1380 yards.

Thereafter, his first win on his big Matchless was in April 1909 and in June 1910 he set the first ever race win at over 75mph, then breaking through the 80mph barrier a month later.

This was to lead to the match races against Jake de Rosier, a visiting rider from America, with his 994cc, chain-driven track-racing Indian machine. After three thrilling two-lap races, the American had won as a result of the decider, at 78.64mph, against Collier's 77.40mph.

Below, Collier is seen being push started for a time trials flying start kilometre in May 1912, to record a speed of 85.38mph.

RAC and Associated Clubs Meeting   29 July 1911

The summer of 1911 featured this typical motor clubmen's event, organised by the RAC and Associated Clubs, the programme of which included two races for motorcycles.

The first was the ACU short-distance handicap over five and a half miles – the equivalent of two laps of the circuit, with the start at the Fork. The field was ready for the off when the unexpected arrival of Prince Henry of Prussia, who wished to meet the competitors, brought the proceedings to a temporary halt.

All got away at the start, although Smith's 499cc Triumph immediately broke its driving belt. The man on scratch, Charlie Collier on his 998 cc Matchless-JAP, was rapidly catching the field until he, too, was put out with driving-belt trouble. The winner of the race, at 54.56mph, was H Hunter, on a 666cc BAT-JAP. Close behind, in second place, came engineer/rider Harry 'Wizard' Martin on his 344cc Martin-JAP.

Third, on a 499cc Triumph, was a very young Malcolm Campbell, later to become famous as a world's record breaker, both on land and water.

The second motorcycle race of the day was for teams entered by clubs affiliated to the ACU. Each team was to be made up of one 500cc single, a 670cc multi-cylinder machine and one sidecar outfit up to 1000cc. All had to be standard touring models as advertised, fully equipped for the road.

The winners were the team representing the Streatham and District MCC and are seen here celebrating their victory. On the left, looking rather pleased with himself, is Sydney Tessier on his twin-cylinder 580cc BAT-JAP. In the middle is W O Oldman, 498cc Zenith-Gradua-JAP and, finally, on the right, A R Hunter on a big 988cc Zenith-Gradua-JAP. It is worth noting, not only the smart attire of Hunter's passenger, but also that ties are worn, even by some riders.

Hundred Mile Record Race   23 September 1911

This was the final event in the BMCRC's last meeting of 1911. The race was over thirty seven laps and was restricted to Classes C, D, and E, up to 500, 750 and 1000cc respectively.

For this race, riders in each class were given different coloured sashes to wear to assist the timekeepers and here we see the new BMCRC secretary, Tom Loughborough, helping riders waiting on the start line with their sashes. He had taken over the post from George Reynolds who had had to stand down due to ill health.

Looking on, already wearing his dark-coloured sash, is the bespectacled Harry Collier with his 998cc Matchless-JAP. As evidenced by the spare belt tied to the forks, his machine is still belt-driven, unlike that of brother Charlie, also in the race, whose similar mount had now been converted to chain drive.

However, few if any of the machines of the period had yet acquired either clutch or gearbox. And, as can be seen by a study of Bell's 580cc BAT-JAP, number 61 in the picture, some were still without any form of front fork springing.

In the race, both Collier brothers failed to finish. Charlie eventually retired with a seized piston whilst, early on, Harry crashed at speed whilst trying to tighten a nut on his carburettor. He was able to get going again, but soon suffered engine trouble and he, too, retired.

The eventual winner, at an average speed of 61.55mph, was amateur rider Jack Haswell on his record-breaking, side-valve 499cc Triumph.

P J WALLACE   499cc Rudge   27 March 1912

The BMCRC's first race meeting of 1912 included a hundred mile race which attracted fifty-five entries. One of these was a newcomer making his debut at the tender age of 16. His name was PJ Wallace, riding a 499cc Rudge.

Happily for us, years later Wallace recalled his first race in a vivid description of what it was like to ride an early motorcycle on the Brooklands Outer Circuit:

"I was already familiar with the starting procedure. With the exhaust-valve lever lifted, you pushed the machine, running hard alongside it until, at the right moment you dropped the lever and, as the engine bursts into life, you leap into the saddle. On the start line, positioned near the middle of thirty or forty other competitors spaced across the whole hundred foot width of the track at the Fork, I tensely awaited the signal to start.

"The notable figure of the chief-starter and timekeeper, Mr A V Ebblewhite, away to the left, extended his arm horizontally. I knew what to do – get away smartly and make a bee-line for the inner edge of the track: the closer one got, the shorter the distance to be covered.

"At last the flag dropped and the scene was transformed. Three dozen young men were heaving their heavy machines forward and running as fast as they could go. There was bedlam. First a few, one after the other, then the whole mass of engines burst into life. As the riders leapt into their saddles, motorcycles swerved dangerously close to one another. As my own engine sprang into life the chap on the right swerved in front, missing my wheel by inches as he made for the inside.

"Once safely in the saddle, all my thoughts of the inside line vanished. Quite apart from the fact that everybody displayed the same intention, my machine bucketed about in the most unexpected manner and it needed every effort to keep it on a straight course. In my innocence I had expected the surface to be quite smooth. The difficulties were accentuated by the need to juggle with the pair of levers controlling the carburettor. Then there was the ignition advance and retard lever which was on the side of the tank about which my knees were tightly gripped anyway.

"As we climbed the one in thirty incline toward the curve around the Members' Hill, most of us were doing about 50 mph. Still much disconcerted to find the going so rough, I came sweeping round the long bend under the Members' Bridge, all the time overshadowed by

the high banking on the right and the hill on the left, and the speed increasing perceptibly.

"Emerging from the hundred foot ravine, there came into view the whole vast expanse of Brooklands stretching far ahead. It was an inspiring moment; it was only a second later when it became yet more memorable but distinctly less inspiring. There came a sudden thrust from the left and, in response, the machine veered to the right, accompanied by a wobbling of the front wheel and handlebars. I was in a cold sweat, heightened by the attainment of maximum speed – about 65 mph – as the bottom of the one in twenty-five incline was passed. Beginning the long straight beside the railway embankment the machine became more stable and the bumps less troublesome.

"The temporary deviation had been caused by the sudden exposure to a south west wind on emerging from the shelter of the Members' Banking. The wind that day was relatively light, its effect much exaggerated by my own stupidity. It was a regulation that motorcycles should carry on each side a twelve inch circular disc, painted black, and bearing the competitor's number in bold white figures. A man with a brush and a bucket of whitewash was posted in the Paddock for this particular duty.

"In my inexperience, I had bolted my number plates to the front forks with the result that even a moderate wind pressure had produced a marked turning-movement on the front wheel assembly.

"The journey down the Railway straight was not marked by any similar untoward event; which was just as well because there was plenty to do. The motorcycles of those days depended upon the operation of a hand-pump for their lubrication; failure in its proper operation could result in engine seizure causing a serious skid or even the rider being thrown over the handlebars. At touring speeds one pumpful every ten miles would normally be sufficient. At racing speed very much more because so much oil was being thrown out of the exhaust. Operation of the pump meant taking one hand off the handlebars. Not too bad if the pump returned with the action of a spring. The more common type with a two-way cock was a nightmare, needing four consecutive operations taking twenty seconds. Hitting one of the bad bumps with one hand off the handlebars was a combination of events to be avoided.

"After the Railway straight came the long, almost semi-circular curve of the Byfleet Banking; it seemed almost interminable. Soon the aeroplane sheds and hangers were visible just beyond the inside edge. I had never seen them before and this was hardly the time to enjoy the view. Then came the narrow bridge over the track which gave access to the flying ground. After passing that the circuit was monotonous, apart from the discomfort.

"At last the banking came to an end and the Fork could be seen ahead: its passing would register the end of the first lap, which has taken less than three minutes. To a spectator, the sections both before and after the Fork might well appear to line in a straight line. In fact, they formed a slightly re-entrant curve, just noticeable on a motor cycle doing 60mph. In a car doing twice that speed it could be a moment of anxiety aiming for the best point of approach to the Members' Banking.

"The problem was accentuated by the presence of one of the worst bumps in the whole course, the other being at the end of the Members' Banking where the course spanned the River Wey. Here some of the really fast machines would take off for nearly fifty yards.

"In my case, the first lap had seen the mass of other competitors diffused into a long line. Being in line and usually close to the inner edge, one saw little ahead beyond the man immediately in front except on the Byfleet Banking where one could see across to other riders curving off to the left. It was only after a few more laps that the really fast machines came by as they lapped me. At about the ninth or tenth lap, apart from feeling tired, I had really settled down. Then, without warning, there came a stunning blow on my back, my machine went into a skid and stopped abruptly, chucking me onto the verge. The driving belt had snapped and become wedged between the belt-rim and the frame. This was toward the end of the Railway straight and, on the long, hot push round the circuit to the Fork, I had ample opportunity to observe my competitors in action.

"Far and away the fastest was one Arthur Moorhouse riding a V-twin, 1000cc Indian. With unfailing regularity he would pass about half-way up the banking and in so doing would break the existing one-hour record. At the next meeting, the following month, he met his death along the Railway Straight by hitting a telegraph post in which remained the imprint of his goggles. The cause was never established.

"By the time I reached the Fork, hot and tired, I was in the company of other unfortunates pushing their machines. The pushers were an assorted lot, two professionals and the rest, like me, amateurs, all inspired by the indomitable spirit of Brooklands - the determination to try again and do better next time".

S F GARRETT 499cc Regal-Green-Precision sidecar 12 October 1912

Sydney Garrett commenced his racing career at Brooklands in early July 1912 on one of the then new 499cc Regal-Green-Precision sidecar outfits. The engine was a water-cooled unit designed and built by the locally based engineer, Frank Baker, who had worked for a time in the American motorcycle industry before returning to England to set up his successful proprietary Precision engine manufacturing company close to Brooklands.

At the Motor Cycling Club's annual meeting in July, Garrett was to come second in an open handicap race for sidecars over four laps. Later that month, he entered a 500cc senior scratch race, this time in solo mode, finishing in second place behind the Singer works rider, G E 'Wizard' Stanley.

At the BMCRC open championship meeting in October, after the start had been delayed by fog, Garrett, seen here back in the sidecar class, had just come third in a hard fought hour race up to 1000cc in which the passengers had to weigh over ten stones! First and second places were snatched by Freddie Barnes and Billy Wells,

998cc Zenith-Gradua-JAP and 994cc Indian respectively. Garrett's distance of 50 miles and 1740 yards was a new 500cc class record.

The last BMCRC meeting of 1912 saw Garrett with a first and second place in the early races of the day, then being denied first place in the final race due to a timekeeper's error. His protest was turned down by the stewards and the win, by just eight yards, awarded to Oliver Godfrey on his 497cc Indian sidecar.

Throughout 1913 Garrett persevered with the Regal-Green-Precision outfit, always being there or thereabouts amongst the top men. At the first BMCRC meeting in March 1914, on the other hand, Garrett appeared on a solo 994cc DOT-JAP, coming second in his first race on the unfamiliar machine. In the last race of the day he came home an easy winner.

Finally, after a brief excursion on a solo 499cc BSA the following June, Garrett turned up at the Motor Cycling Club's July meeting on a big 994cc Indian, promptly winning the event's 1000cc three-lapper, this being his last race before the war brought proceedings at the track to a halt.

G E STANLEY   299cc Singer   12 October 1912

Stanley made an unusual choice for his debut on a motorcycle at Brooklands, entering his 499cc Premier in the same sixty-lap, l64 mile marathon race in June 1910 as did Fitzherbert (page 30).

It was also an inauspicious introduction for, on the third lap, Stanley's tank filler cap shook loose and disappeared on the track, drenching him in petrol. As this happened down on the Railway Straight, it was a long and uncomfortable push round the circuit back to the pit area at the Fork, where he was only too glad to retire.

During the ensuing year, Stanley had become a Singer works rider and was entered for the first time on a 499cc Singer in the two races at the June 1911 BARC meeting, taking second place in the first race and winning the second.

This was the start of Stanley's long succession of wins at Brooklands for the Singer Company and he was soon to become their principal rider.

In early 1912, another rider had been testing a revolutionary, Louis Coatalen-designed Singer 499cc engine having four valves and a water-cooled detachable head. However, Stanley was now finding so much speed from the reliable old side-valve 499cc engine that the new engine was never to appear on the track. Amply justifying this decision, in May 1912 Stanley set a new record in Class C on the side-valve machine at a speed of 75.45mph over the f/s kilometre. He also won the following 500cc scratch race at an average speed of 65.93mph.

That autumn, Stanley was concentrating on several more records, taking the Class C fifty miles at 68.70mph, finishing as darkness fell. Two days later he added to Singer's bag a new flying-start five mile record at over 70mph.

Seen here, on 12 October, having won a race 'just to keep in trim', this time on a 299cc Singer, it was back to the Coventry works to prepare for an attack on the 500cc hour record a few days later. The attempt was successful, although towards the end of the run the machine's inlet valve broke. Despite slowing the pace, the engine continued to run intermittently and Stanley took the record at 67 miles 782 yards. Remarkably, the side-valved Singer was pulling a 3.78 to 1, single gear belt drive.

The following year, now on a 349cc machine, Stanley was entered in The Great Six Hour Race on Wednesday 16 July 1913. Having led his class for the first hour, it was announced he had become the first rider of a 350 to cover more than sixty miles in the hour. Sadly, after just one more hour, his rear tyre was worn through to the canvas and he retired, simply saying, with a shrug, that he'd "had enough"!

H GIBSON   554cc Bradbury sidecar   October 1912

Bradbury motorcycles appeared intermittently at Brooklands between 1910 and 1913 and enjoyed some success in the hands of Hugh Gibson.

In the picture Gibson, kneeling on the left, is seen at a pit stop during a race in October 1912. His passenger, hidden by the machine, is clearly making an adjustment requiring the use of the open-ended spanner lying on the concrete. The bowler-hatted crew member is filling the petrol tank, overseen by one of the ever present fire attendants provided by the Pyrene fire extinguisher company.

In November 1912, Gibson set new two hour and 100 mile records for sidecars up to 750cc, at speeds of 45.99 and 46.04mph respectively.

He also was to take part in the famous six hour race during the BMCRC's fifth meeting of 1913, with a field of no less than fifty riders and drivers on solo machines, sidecars and three-wheeled cyclecars.

Three hours into this marathon, Gibson had covered 48 laps and was running in second place in Class H, sidecars up to 750cc, only three laps behind the experienced E B Ware on his much more powerful 750cc Zenith-Gradua.

When the flag fell at the end of the gruelling six hours, Gibson had completed 82 laps, a total of 227 miles, at an average speed of 37.80mph. He still finished in second place in his class, only trailing the winner, Ware, by fourteen laps.

The apparently modest speeds are best judged by considering that the figures took into account the regular stops for fuel, oil and mechanical adjustments – often a replacement tyre as well. Both rider and passenger would clearly have needed such breaks, however brief, during the rough and noisy ride.

The wickerwork sidecar body in the picture is typical of the period and would probably have been fitted for Gibson's entry in the six hour race the following July. It was not unknown in those early days for a sidecar body of this type to give best to the pounding from the legendary bumpy concrete surface, the wickerwork gradually becoming unravelled, no doubt to the alarm of the occupant.

500cc Sidecar Scratch Race 14 June 1913

Run on Saturday, 14 June 1913, the BMCRC's fourth members' meeting featured ten three lap scratch races, including this one, for sidecar outfits up to 500cc.

There were five entrants for this race: Sydney Garrett, 499cc Regal-Green-Precision sidecar; Freddie Barnes, on one of his own products, a Zenith-Gradua sidecar with 493cc JAP engine; Folwell's 499cc BSA sidecar; and two more Zenith-Gradua outfits, but with 499cc Green-Precision engines, ridden by H C Mills and H Riddell.

The Green-Precision engines in three of the entries, designed and manufactured locally by Frank Baker, were unusual in that they were water-cooled, the two radiators being fitted, pannier-fashion, one on each side of the single cylinder.

For this race, pushers were allowed, rather than the more usual expedient of a joint effort by the rider and passenger. In this instance, up to three pushers had been roped in for the start, the passenger of one outfit being seen to add his weight before, at the last second, diving aboard.

Garrett had established a lead going into the second of the three laps, holding it to the end of the race with a winning speed of 48.39mph.

In the picture, coming off the banking under the Members' Bridge soon after the Fork start, Folwell's BSA is in the foreground, with Garrett on the left, followed by Barnes. Folwell is leaning over to his left to keep the inside wheel from lifting at this point on the bend. There is no sign so far of the remaining two competitors.

From the postures of the passengers it is possible to imagine their discomfort. At least in these early days they could see where they were going. That is assuming that they wanted to. In later years, in the 'coffin', wind-cheating sidecars, the passenger would be mostly lying prone, and facing backwards. We illustrate this type of 'chair' on page 252.

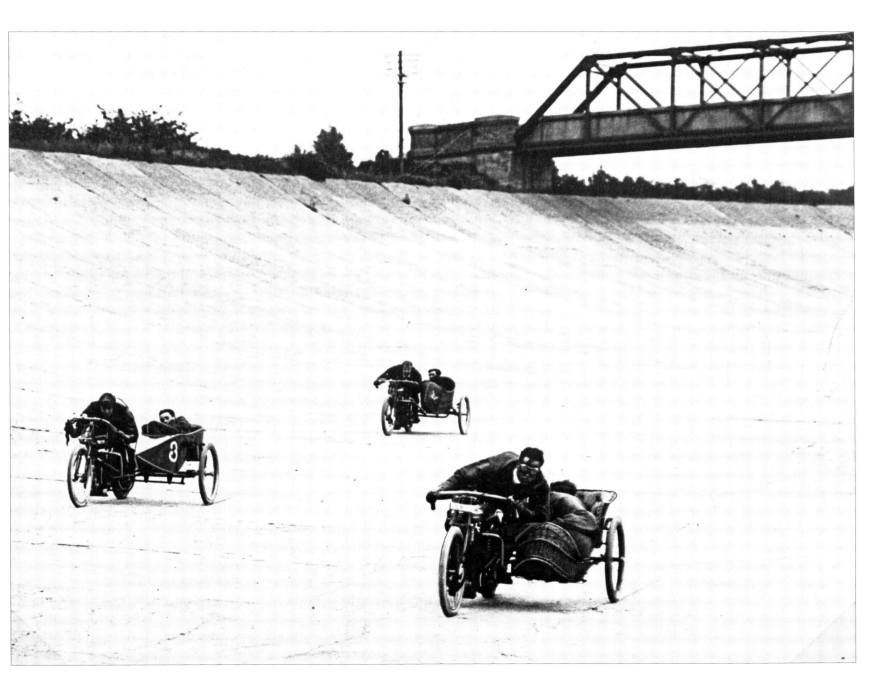

The Great Six Hour Race   16 July 1913

The BMCRC had announced a marathon six hour, multi-class scratch race to be run at the Club's fifth meeting of 1913 as one of Brookland's leading events of the year. It was devised primarily to give all taking part the opportunity to set new class records.

Temporary pits were set up at the Fork and stops would only be allowed for refuelling and repair. All machines were to be clearly numbered, as opposed to the commonly used system of riders' numbers being whitewashed on their backs.

The massed start from scratch of the fifty entrants was dramatic, the dense clouds of smoke emitted by the two-stroke Scotts of Wood and Applebee causing confusion amongst following riders. The early stages of the race were inevitably dominated by the big Matchless and Indian machines, closely followed by the Singers of Cocker and Stanley. Surprisingly, the smoke-emitting Scott of Tim Wood was soon to be lapping in sixth place.

Before long the temporary pits were becoming busy and early retirements included Freddie Barnes and A V Sumner on their Zenith-Graduas. Another Zenith, ridden by Albert Knight, skidded violently into the pit, fell over and burst into flame. The Pyrene extinguisher attendant, as always, dealt quickly with the problem and Knight was soon back in the running. Another machine had been on fire and was retired. After numerous other alarms, excursions and changes of fortune, including the disintegration of a sidecar body, to the obvious concern of its inhabitant, the end of the marathon was flagged at 5.30pm, no doubt to the relief of many of the surviving competitors.

The winners in the solo classes were Mason (350cc NUT-JAP), Haswell (499cc Triumph), McNab (745cc Trump-JAP) and Cookson (986cc Matchless-JAP). In the three classes for sidecars and three-wheel cyclecars, the winners were Riddell (499cc Zenith-Gradua-Green-Precision), Ware (750cc Zenith-Gradua-JAP) and Holder (986cc Morgan-Blomfield). G W Hands won the 1100cc four-wheeled cyclecar class driving a 1088 cc Calthorpe.

The team prize was won by Enfield, yet another success for the 350cc V-twins. Class records were set up by a number of riders, amongst them Haswell on his Triumph and Stanley (Singer). It should be mentioned that Bert le Vack came third in Class C on his 496cc Motosacoche.

The Enfield Team   350cc Enfield V-twins   13 September 1913

The BMCRC's monthly meeting on Saturday, 13 September 1913 saw a large programme of races running to time.

After the traditional record time trials which opened the day, a series of one lap sprint races for solo, sidecar and cyclecar classes was followed by the senior one hour team race. This was for teams of three identical machines of the same make under 1000cc. Four teams were entered, Enfield, Rudge, Triumph and Indian.

Despite having the smallest capacity machines, at 350cc, the consistent and reliable running of all three V-twin Enfields, seen in the picture, gave the team the greatest aggregate mileage overall and thus the team prize. The riders were, from left to right, H W Colver, H Greaves and D Iron.

Known to one and all as Bert, Colver had been a regular member of the Colliers' Matchless team since 1905, only standing down in 1911.

He had returned to racing, on an Enfield 350cc V-twin, in the recent Great Six Hour Race in July, finishing second in his class.

Greaves rode Enfield machines from the outset. At first competing at Brooklands on a 425cc Enfield single in 1912, he joined Colver in the 350cc V-twin Enfield team for the six hour race the following year. He then competed on 350s right through to the last BMCRC meeting before the war, on 25 July 1914.

The last of the three, Iron, on the right, was the last to join the Enfield team, taking part, with Bert Colver, in a ten-mile race for 350cc solo machines in August,1913. For his next outing he was in the team race pictured here. In June the following year, after a brief adventure with a 986cc Matchless, Iron was reunited with the 350cc Enfield V-twin for his last appearance at Brooklands, when, at high speed, the Enfield's rear tyre blew off the rim.

E F REMINGTON   986cc Matchless-JAP   18 October 1913

Eric Remington rode a big Matchless from the very start of his racing career at Brooklands. His first outing, at the Whit Monday BARC meeting in May 1912, was not encouraging, however, his machine being reluctant to start and throwing away its driving belt when it did.

Remington's name is absent from the race reports throughout that summer, but re-emerges in a very dramatic way at the last BARC meeting in September.

In the only motorcycle race on the card, the short-distance handicap over two laps, Remington on his Matchless was the first across the finishing line. Unfortunately, his brake failed and he went straight up the Members' Banking and over the top. He was unhurt and the only real damage to his machine was that both wheels were buckled. Despite winning the race at nearly 74 mph, Remington was disqualified by the stewards for not having stopped within the prescribed distance!

Still keeping faith with the Matchless-JAP for 1913, Remington scored his first win at the June BMCRC meeting, in a 1000cc scratch race, now running on benzole. A win in a ten mile 1000cc race in August also gave him the fastest lap at over 80mph. This was followed by a second place the following month.

Speeds were increasing in all classes during 1913. At the BMCRC championship meeting in October, Remington recorded fastest time of the day in the record time trials, with an average speed for the flying start kilometre of 85.38mph. He also won the final race of the day, the five-lap 'Motor Car Journal Challenge Cup', at a speed of 76.43mph.

Unaccountably, Remington had switched to a 986cc NUT-JAP for 1914, on which he only enjoyed modest success during the year. Once again, as in 1912, he made headlines in every sense when, at the BARC Whit Monday meeting, the front forks of his big machine broke at over 70 mph and he fell heavily.

Happily, as he was wearing a helmet he again escaped virtually unhurt. The wearing of helmets had not yet become compulsory, but incidents such as this would in due course persuade the ACU at least to lay down guidelines.

J EMERSON   498cc ABC   13 January 1914

Jack Emerson had shaken up the Brooklands habitués when he turned up for the BMCRC 500cc seniors' race in September 1912. Apparently he had ridden his 490cc Norton all the way down from Hull earlier in the week and, in practice, was lapping consistently at 68mph. At face value, it was the old familiar long-stroke, side-valve Norton, without clutch or gearbox and driven by belt to the back wheel.

In the race, Emerson ran away from the field and, at the finish, some fifty five laps later, was almost a quarter of an hour ahead of the second man, Haswell on his 499cc Triumph. Emerson's average speed for the race was 63.88mph.

He had then joined Granville Bradshaw's All British Engine Company as the works tester, and, during 1913, had been kept busy on a project based on the new ohv ABC already on sale to the public. This was to be an attempt on the 500cc flying start kilometre and mile records currently held by Singer.

To the specially prepared machine Emerson had attached a thirty inch long conical tail, constructed from light timber strips and covered with aeroplane fabric. This primitive form of streamlining probably contributed to his success, taking both records with speeds of 80.47mph over the kilometre and 78.26mph for the mile. In the small picture, Emerson shows off his device, somewhat self-consciously, perhaps.

The extraordinarily clear picture on the right is of the Granville Bradshaw-designed 498cc ABC flat-twin machine on which Jack Emerson had become the first rider officially to exceed 80mph on a half-litre motorcycle. The flat twin engine had a bore and stroke of 70.4mm by 64mm with push-rod operated overhead valves and steel cylinders. Transmission was by chain to a countershaft, thence by belt to the back wheel. Later plans included chain final drive.

BARC Brooklands Race Meeting 1 June 1914

By now, the more important motor race meetings put on by the BARC included one or two races for motorcycles, and the 1914 Whit Monday meeting was no exception.

The prize money at these events was always generous, due to the thousands of spectators drawn through the turnstiles for big BARC car meetings, as compared with the BMCRC motorcycle-only meetings which attracted comparatively few spectators.

The prize money attracted large entries for the two motorcycle races, the first of which, the short motorcycle handicap over two laps, had no less than forty three entrants. Of these, only two riders were allowed assistance from pushers for the Fork Start; one because of an injured knee, the other having a stiff leg!

Usually two lap races tended to be rather tame affairs. In this case, however, the handicappers had got it just right, the two leading men at the end of the last lap being neck and neck, Eddie Kickham on his 349cc Douglas just pipping Holzapfel's 347cc Regal-Green-Precision, as seen in the picture on the far right.

It was during practice for this race that E F Remington had the front forks of his big NUT-JAP break off at over 70 mph, the rider escaping virtually unhurt as related on page 58 .

The photograph of the finish of the race illustrates the large number of spectators who would turn out for big BARC car meetings, especially on Bank Holidays. The obvious interest shown by the people in the picture could equally well be due to bets placed on the race with the Brooklands bookies as with the excitement of the close finish.

MCC's Annual Meeting   18 July 1914

Later in the summer, a decent crowd turned up for the Motor Cycling Club's annual event which always featured several races. Seen in the left-hand picture is F J Ellis on his 347cc Royal Enfield on the Byfleet Banking about to win the Clubs' Invitation Dispatch Race. He was a member of the Woolwich and Plumstead MCC.

Perhaps more exciting was the later race in which the Matchless works rider Bert Colver found his team colleague Charlie Collier in winning form, losing to him by a few yards.

More significantly, although probably unnoticed at the time, was that the 350-560cc three lap race was won by Herbert le Vack, riding a 496cc Motosacoche, and so registering his first ever race win at Brooklands.

J P Le GRAND   348cc Singer   1 June 1914

J P Le Grand is seen here on his belt-driven Singer having come third in the second of two motorcycle races in the BARC Whit Monday meeting described on the previous page.

Le Grand and his friend W A Jacobs shared a common interest in motorcycle racing at Brooklands and both competed at the track from early 1909 until 1914. They were never to set any records there but they could be said to represent the best of the amateur element of the early Brooklands tradition.

They first appeared on 3.5hp (500cc) Rex machines at the BARC Easter meeting of 1909, when two races for motorcycles were included. Le Grand came out again on his Rex in the Easter meeting the following year but, again, did not appear in the results.

Indeed, neither of the friends appears in press reports until 1913 when, at the Essex MC race meeting on 24 May, both were entered, now on 348cc Singers. In the two lap all comers open handicap, Le Grand took the win, with Jacobs half a machine's length behind in second place.

The two are next seen at the BARC's mid - summer meeting on Saturday 21 June. On this occasion, only Jacobs figured in the results: a third place, so earning himself a fiver, awarded by The Daily Express. This was an instance of the comparatively big prize money available at BARC car race meetings. An equivalent third place at the more poorly supported BMCRC motorcycle events might earn you a pound; more likely, a little cup for the mantelpiece.

At the Motor Cycling Club's big annual meeting in June 1913, both Singer riders did well, Jacobs winning a two lap handicap for 350cc machines with Le Grand taking third place. In the main race of the day, Le Grand finished hard on the heels of the winner, Harry Collier (496cc Matchless-MAG) with Jacobs close behind.

We next find them at the BARC Easter meeting in April 1914. Now both on 248cc Singers, they took first and second places in the 250cc class flying start kilometre time trials with speeds of 57.36 and 53.77mph respectively.

Thereafter, at a meeting on Whit Monday, Le Grand registered a third place, whilst, in July, Jacobs won a three lap 350cc handicap race, Le Grand dropping out with tyre trouble.

And finally, on Bank Holiday Monday in August 1914, the last BARC meeting before 1920, Le Grand withdrew with carburettor problems and a cracked piston.

The following day, Britain was at war.

C B FRANKLIN   998cc Indian   17 June 1914

In 1910 Charlie Franklin was one of the first riders to be signed up by W H 'Billy' Wells, the agent for Indian Motor Cycles in Britain. Coming third in his very first race at Brooklands, the 60 lap TT race, Franklin was to join battle with the Collier brothers on their big Matchless-JAPs for the next four years .

By 1912, now mounted on the overhead inlet valve, 998 cc V-twin Indian machine, Franklin interspersed racing with record breaking over distances up to 350 miles – some 130 laps of Brooklands uneven circuit. He also regularly entered sidecar races, as indeed did most of the professional riders of the day.

It was said that Franklin's colleagues believed he had inadvertently discovered the so-called 'squish' effect, to create turbulence in the combustion chamber of an engine and thus an increase in power.

Apparently he had welded a piece of metal on the underside of his engine's cylinder head in the hope of raising the compression. This may have produced a Ricardo-type combustion space, pre-dating, it was suggested, by ten years the work of Sir Harry.

The photograph on the right shows just one example of how Brooklands was often used as an open air showcase for the more sales-conscious manufacturers, in this instance Indian Motor Cycles, set up by Billy Wells, the one with arms akimbo and wearing a cap.

The date was 17 June 1914, and Franklin was to make an attempt on the 1000cc twenty-four hour record, which stood to Harry Collier.

The attempt was destined to end dramatically after only three hours. At full speed, the eight-valve machine caught fire after a petrol pipe broke. Franklin was enveloped in flames which he managed to put out by rolling on the trackside grass. The machine was a write-off.

After a while another Indian was produced and, on that one, Franklin managed to set a new 1000cc standing start ten mile record, previously held by E F Remington, like Collier, riding a works Matchless. On the Indian, Franklin's new record speed was 77.95 mph.

The carefully staged group seen here shows Franklin flanked by Billy Wells and, wearing the Indian-inscribed sweater, team rider Oliver Godfrey. The Brooklands chief timekeeper, E V Ebblewhite, is comfortably ensconced in an obviously showroom-prepared Indian sidecar outfit. Whether the set-up is before or after the accident is open to conjecture.

O L de LISSA 496cc Motosacoche sidecar 18 July 1914

Osborne Louis de Lissa is pictured here on his road equipped, twin-cylinder Motosacoche outfit, having won a three lap handicap race for sidecars at the Motor Cycling Club's sixth annual meeting on 18 July 1914. In the sidecar is his protégé Bert Le Vack who, at the same meeting, had won his very first race at Brooklands, also on a Motosacoche.

De Lissa had taken charge of the British end of the Swiss motorcycle engine company in 1908, and had sold more of the firm's 1.25hp engines in his first three months 'on the road' than had been sold in the previous three years. Having retained the services of the experienced trials and TT rider J S Holroyd, who won a Gold Medal for Motosacoche in the 1910 Scottish Trial, both would appear regularly at Brooklands driving Motosacoche sidecar outfits.

Becoming managing director of the British company in 1913, and having taken on Le Vack as his engine development engineer, de Lissa persuaded the Geneva factory to extend its range of proprietory engines, in particular those of larger capacity. These were to include the Le Vack-inspired 496cc V-twin and all would now be sold under de Lissa's newly named MAG engine company. The small capacity units were to be manufactured by the Royal Enfield company under a licencing agreement set up by de Lissa.

He himself had brought out a number of innovations for motorcycles, such as a drive-belt connecting hook, produced for him by Terrys of Redditch, an air-cooled exhaust valve and a simplified expanding-pulley gearing device. He patented at least two of these designs

By now affectionately known to the whole Brooklands community as Ollie, de Lissa continued to promote his company's products by regular and often successful appearances at Brooklands driving Motosacoche sidecar outfits, still occasionally with Le Vack as passenger, right up to the middle twenties.

E B WARE   744cc Morgan -JAP cyclecar   25 July 1914

E B Ware was to become one of Brooklands' most successful cyclecar exponents, always to the fore with his JAP-powered, three-wheel Morgans. In the beginning, however, he was to get the feel of the track in 1910 on a motorcycle, a King's Own, with 964cc JAP engine. However, despite it having such rare luxuries, in those days, of chain drive and a two-speed gearbox, he failed at first to impress.

For the following two seasons he favoured a Zenith-Gradua-JAP sidecar, gaining experience and some better results. In 1914, he added a Morgan-JAP cyclecar to his stable, for a while entering both machines at race meetings.

On 25 July 1914, at the last BMCRC meeting before the 1914-18 war, Ware set a new 750cc cyclecar f/s kilometre record, at 65.10mph, and we see him, on the opposite page, in his body-hugging Morgan, rightly pleased with his record, the first of many to come.

After the war, he was to reappear with a much modified Morgan, with larger 1098cc JAP engine, more complete bodywork and disc wheels. Still keeping his hand in with a 347cc NUT-JAP, he continued to chase records in the bigger-engined Morgan to some effect, in April 1921 taking the f/s kilometre record for 1100 cc cyclecars to 77.67mph, then, six months later, improving that to 86.04mph. To this he added the f/s 5 mile and s/s 10 mile records in the same class.

Now employed by the JAP engine concern as development engineer, he found his own racing activities to be somewhat curtailed, although still bringing the Morgan out from time to time.

In September 1924, Ware had entered the machine in the Junior Car Club's 200 mile car race. With the JAP-supported motorcycle rider Tommy Allchin (see page 150) on board as his passenger, Ware was soon lapping the Morgan consistently at around 90mph. Then, coming off the Byfleet Banking, his rear tyre threw its tread, becoming trapped in a driving chain and jamming the wheel. The Morgan crashed heavily, throwing both men on to the track. Allchin was not badly hurt but Ware was severely injured, having to spend the next two years in hospital.

Eventually, his enthusiasm for motorised sport undimmed, he joined the Auto-Cycle Union, ultimately serving in the capacities of steward, scrutineer and speedway engineer.

Combined Armed Services Meeting   7 August 1915

Early in 1915, the BMCRC had realised that any plans they may have had for club activities that year would have to be reconsidered in the light of both practical and moral issues.

In the first place the track had already suffered badly from the many solid-tyred Royal Flying Corps lorries now based at Brooklands. The other important consideration was that the public would not countenance such trivialities as civilian motorised sport with the country at war.

On the other hand, with D R O'Donovan still finding the Railway Straight relatively smooth, at least sufficiently so to carry on his Norton tuning and record breaking business, thoughts turned to staging, not a civilian, but a military-based event for that summer. Indeed, the idea had already been suggested in a letter to 'The Motor Cycle' from an Army officer.

Accordingly, plans were laid for a Combined Services Meeting, to take place on Saturday 7 August 1915. The day's programme was to consist of eleven competitive events, including half-mile sprints on the Railway Straight, hill-climbs on the Test Hill, and 'quick-change plug' and 'serpentine slow' races. All competitors were to be in uniform and drawn from all branches of the armed services.

On the day, no fewer than 172 motorcycles of all types were entered and the fine weather helped the Club run the event without a hitch. Despite some misgivings over safety due to the lack of public enclosures along the Railway Straight, it was decided to admit spectators in view of the special nature of the event In the picture on the right, a competitor on the Test Hill is closely watched by a critical audience.

Such a success was this first Services meeting that a second one was laid on for the following September, receiving 195 entries. A similar event in October planned as a morale booster for the workers at the Royal Aircraft Factory at Farnborough attracted a huge entry of no less than 245 motorcycles, with spectators turning out in large numbers.

The First Post-War Meeting   Easter Monday 5 April 1920

During the war Brooklands had been temporarily handed over to the Royal Flying Corps and the constant use of solid-tyred Thornycroft and Leyland lorries had played havoc with the concrete track and service areas.

After hostilities ceased the War Department had begun to live up to its commitment to make good the damage. But the work took so long to complete that it was not possible to recommence racing until April 1920. Even then the track would never be quite the same again.

So it was that the first post-war meeting, a joint BARC and BMCRC event, was scheduled for Easter Monday, 5 April, but heavy rain in the morning led to the decision to postpone the meeting proper until the following Saturday.

One of those entered for the meeting was Harry Martin, seen here in the rain on his old 489cc Matchless-MAG. Martin was one of the few pre-war riders to reappear on the track in the twenties: many had clearly not survived the war.

One who had, Jack Woodhouse, was a RFC pilot. He is seen here, in uniform, standing in the background. He was also entered in the now abandoned race, to ride his big 994cc Matchless-MAG. Aware of the disappointment of the huge crowds that had turned up, Woodhouse took the opportunity of the weather relenting slightly to challenge Capt. Malcolm Campbell, who had brought along his 15 litre Lorraine-Dietrich car, to a match race, which Campbell just won, at a speed of 78.90mph.

After lunch conditions were much improved, and so, to celebrate the re-opening, everyone took to the track, in more than five hundred vehicles of every sort and size.

H Le VACK 496cc Duzmo 5 April 1920

Another rider hoping to have taken part in the first post-war race meeting at Brooklands was Herbert Le Vack, now thirty three years old, who had cut his racing teeth on a Motosacoche machine before the war.

He was intending to ride this Duzmo, an oddly named machine built by John Wallace, one of the many young engineers becoming aware of the potential of the emerging motorcycle industry.

Up until 1914 Le Vack had been involved in England with the design of engines for the Swiss Motosacoche concern. Now he had joined Wallace in producing the 89x70mm, 496cc overhead valve engine for the Duzmo. The head was detachable and both head and barrel were held down on the crankcase by four long bolts.

Robbed of the opportunity, like everyone else, of enjoying this first post-war competitive outing, Le Vack was due to turn out again on the new machine the following Saturday. However he is listed in the press report of the day as being a non-starter.

Later in the summer, Le Vack was competing at the Liverpool speed trials, and it was his performance at that event that finally led to Billy Wells, the Indian Motor Cycle Company's agent in Britain, signing up Le Vack as a works rider for the rest of the season and for 1921.

The Victory Race Meeting   10 April 1920

For the first proper post-war race meeting, postponed from the previous wet Easter Monday, a big crowd once again turned out, this time in dry weather conditions.

The first event of the day was the Victory Handicap, over three laps, for solo machines of any class. The start was at the Fork, competitors then passing the Fork twice more before entering the Finishing Straight and dashing for the Long Finishing Line.

The big field for the first race is seen here assembling in the Paddock. Prominent in the line-up can be seen A F Houlberg on his new and unfamiliar-looking 345cc Wooler.

This machine had immediately, and rather unkindly, acquired the nickname of the 'Flying Banana' on account of the bright yellow paintwork on the fuel tank, which projected around and beyond the steering head. The Wooler was, however, quite advanced for its day, having plunger front and rear suspension and being powered by a horizontally-opposed inlet over exhaust, flat-twin engine mounted longitudinally, high in the frame.

The winner of this, the first motorcycle race at Brooklands after the 1914-18 war, was Jack Emerson on his little 396cc ABC, as described in more detail over the page.

J EMERSON   396cc ABC   10 April 1920

The winner of the Victory Handicap, the first race at Brooklands after the 1914-18 war, was Jack Emerson riding this little 396 cc flat-twin engined ABC. His winning speed was 66.7mph.

As we have already seen, Emerson had been the All British Engine Company's works test rider since well before the war. He had been involved in the development of Grenville Bradshaw's new model even before the outbreak of hostilities, so that the appearance of the replacement of the earlier 498 cc ABC at the Victory Race Meeting was something of a coup; especially so as it proved to be in winning form.

Bradshaw's new machine was made at the Kingston-upon-Thames factory of the Sopwith Aviation and Engineering Company, which had been building fighter aircraft during the war. Weighing only 175 lbs, the new model differed from its 498cc pre-war brothers by having its flat-twin engine set across, rather than in line with, the lightweight frame. The cylinders had a bore and stroke of 68 x 57mm, with concave pistons. In unit with the engine was a four-speed gearbox, the final drive being by chain, whilst the frame and forks were sprung by means of quarter-elliptic leaf springs.

The machine also possessed an almost unheard of luxury in those days: automatic lubrication. This was a real boon, in racing in particular, as it was no longer necessary to take one hand off the handlebars at speed in order to pump oil to the engine.

It has often been suggested that this model of the ABC could be regarded as the predecessor of the BMW. However, in the event, Sopwiths were to put the new ABC on the market before the design had been fully developed, and, by 1921, the company was in liquidation.

J WOODHOUSE   992cc Matchless-MAG   10 April 1920

Already seen in RFC uniform at the earlier, rained-off first post-war race meeting, Woodhouse was more suitably attired for the re-run the following Saturday.

A close friend of the Collier family, owners of the successful Matchless factory, Woodhouse had been given this 992cc, 8-valve, V-twin Matchless-MAG machine by Charlie Collier. Here he was to put the machine to good use in the one lap solo sprint, winning easily at a speed of 75.9mph.

It is interesting to see that Woodhouse had fitted a mudguard to the front wheel, no doubt in case of wet conditions such as previously.

Brooklands was challenging enough in the dry, without having to peer through a curtain of spray thrown up from an unprotected front wheel.

The MAG engine in the Matchless would have been built under licence from the Swiss company Motosacoche, by whom Herbert Le Vack had been employed in England as a design engineer in the years leading up to the war.

Woodhouse only made a handful of outings during the next two years; then he disappears from the race reports. Perhaps, in view of his recent experiences with the Royal Flying Corps, he decided that he had had plenty enough excitement, at least for the time being.

V GAYFORD   680cc Zenith-Gradua-JAP   10 July 1920

In blustery weather, with intermittent showers, the Motor Cycling Club's first post-war race meeting on 10 July 1920 attracted many well-known riders eager to blow away the cobwebs after a six year break from racing.

However the first race of the day was to be won by newcomer Victor Gayford on his 680cc Zenith-Gradua-JAP, breaking his duck in the three lap 500-1000cc handicap, at 62.6mph. He probably benefitted from the handicapper's generosity to a new boy.

At a BMCRC members' meeting a week later, Gayford was further encouraged by a third place in a ten mile 750cc scratch race, behind Porter's 396cc ABC and Victor Horsman's 490cc side-valve Norton.

The following month, on 14 August, at the meeting organised jointly by the BMCRC and Essex Motor Club, the really big names were on hand: Remington, Baldwin, Harveyson, Emerson, Le Vack and Don, amongst others. Gayford was entered in the three lap senior open handicap for solo machines over 500cc. After a good start Gayford was lying second until overwhelmed firstly by Bert Le Vack's 994cc eight-valve Indian and then Oliver Baldwin's 986cc Matchless-JAP. As Le Vack crossed the Long Finishing Line to

win, his Indian caught fire, a conflagration that was quickly put out by the Pyrene man.

Victor Gayford must have been thrilled to come third in a race in such company only three weeks after his first appearance at the track, especially following home the likes of Le Vack and Baldwin. However, being close behind at the finish, he could not have helped but witness Le Vack's fiery misfortune. Perhaps this was one reason why he is not to be seen again at Brooklands.

Pictured here after his first win, Gayford poses on his Zenith. The layout of the patented Gradua gear, invented in 1907 by the Zenith designer, Freddie Barnes, can be seen quite clearly.

The gear gave a range of ratios from 3.5:1 to 9:1. Ratios were changed by means of the coffee mill-type handwheel on top of the tank, operating a system of rods and levers which moved the rear wheel backwards and forwards in slotted lugs. At the same time, the engine pulley was expanded or contracted, one flange being keyed to the engine shaft and the other left free to slide, actuated by a quick thread.

Barnes' own victories in the early days with his invention led to Zenith-Graduas being barred from competition by a number of clubs, leading to the famous Zenith 'Barred Gate' tank badge.

S GILL 345cc Alecto 3 August 1920

Made by Cashmore Brothers, of Balham, South London, this Alecto was fitted with their own single cylinder, 345cc deflector type two port, two-stroke engine. An outside flywheel was used, also seen on several other makes of engine, such as Blackburne.

Stanley Gill had brought his belt-driven machine to Brooklands aiming to set up new time and distance records in Class B, 350cc solo motorcycles. On a standard machine, apart from sporting an Amac racing carburettor and being stripped of all non-essentials, Gill succeeded beyond all his expectations.

His haul totalled twenty one records. These included the nine, ten, eleven and twelve hours, and the 400 and 450 mile records in Class B. His time for the 450 miles also represented new records in Class C (500cc) and Class D (750cc). All the records were set at between 41.41 and 42.60mph, being average speeds which of course included all stops for replenishment.

This was the first time that long-distance records had been successfully taken at the track on a two-stroke machine. Cashmore Bros. must have been delighted at the outcome. This was the beginning of the 'cash for records' golden years at Brooklands, when riders and team managers were to become increasingly reliant upon bonus payments for records and race wins which would give exposure to the products used, such as fuel, oil and tyres.

In the case of Gill's success it would be safe to assume that he had involved the Alecto concern at the outset, probably agreeing an appropriate rate of bonus for any new records set; possibly as much as £3 a time. The Amac carburettor would have been provided free of charge, even if only on loan and Gill would have also arrived at some agreement with each of the various suppliers of his consumables.

His record breaking career appears to have begun and ended with the Alecto, for, in the next three years, Gill was to turn to rather more lusty 497cc and 997cc Indians. He was to find that records for machines in these categories would be much harder to achieve.

H Le VACK   994cc Indian   14 August 1920

The first 'open' Brooklands meeting of 1920, jointly organised by the BMCRC and the Essex Motor Club, saw Bert Le Vack make his first appearance on an Indian. The American racing team manager Billy Wells had entered his new signing to ride two machines, a 497cc four-valve single and this fearsome 994cc eight-valve V-twin Indian.

Failing to score in his first race of the day, on the smaller machine, Le Vack transferred to the big V-twin for the three lap senior open handicap race. From a joint scratch start with fellow team member Reuban Harveyson, Le Vack carved his way through the field to win the race at 80mph.

He would remember his debut with the Indian team for the rest of his life due to an unpleasant incident as he crossed the finished line in the second race. In that moment his machine caught fire, leaving him with nasty burns on his legs, which would trouble him in years to come.

Reputedly, this eight-valve V-twin was Charlie Franklin's pre-war racer, perhaps even the very replacement he had to use during the Indian Motor Co. record attempts on 17 June 1914, when his first machine on the day was destroyed by fire (see page 66). Nicknamed the Camel, Le Vack's mount would prove to be a handful on Brooklands' bumpy circuit, control being further compromised by the lack of a throttle, meaning that the engine was either running flat out or not running at all, dependant upon a somewhat unreliable magneto cut-out button.

This photograph must have been taken before Le Vack set out for the start of the race.

R KAYE DON   349cc AJS   9 October 1920

In the 350cc solo scratch race at the BMCRC Championship meeting on 9 October 1920, Kaye Don rode one of the 349cc AJS machines which had triumphed in the 1920 Junior TT in the I o M. Don won the six lap race at 63.78mph, a full lap ahead of Vivian Prestwich on a 349cc NUT-JAP.

Don's AJS was one of the first British motor-cycles with an engine having a hemispherical combustion chamber. The inclined valves were operated by long, inclined pushrods, whilst the detachable iron cylinder head was held down by flexible steel strips attached to each side of the crankcase as well as being tethered to the front down tube of the frame.

The fuel tank was in two bolted halves and the oil tank mounted on the saddle tube. The all-chain transmission had an enclosed primary chain driving a 3-speed countershaft gearbox and two engageable engine sprockets, giving, in effect, six speeds in all.

Don had first appeared at Brooklands early in 1920 when racing at the track was resumed. Riding a single-gear, belt-drive 490cc Norton, he finished second to a Harley-Davidson in a handicap race in June.

The AJS seen here gave him victory on only his second outing at the track. It was one of at least a dozen different machines, with capacities ranging from 248cc to 998cc, which he rode with success during the several seasons he spent racing motorcycles at Brooklands.

Within three years he had also taken up racing cars, cementing his reputation as one of the all time great Brooklands competitors.

R N JUDD 490cc Norton 29 March 1921

Judd had started his Brooklands career in 1920 assisting the amateur rider Dr Maurice Breese to set up middle and long distance records on a belt-driven 348cc Coulson-Blackburne and sidecar. Judd helped out particularly as sidecar passenger and mechanic.

He then joined D R O'Donovan, the well known Norton tuner/rider and was soon busy testing the 490cc Nortons that were to be sold to the public with guaranteed performance, the engines being individually prepared (see page 100). During this time Judd covered the flying start kilometre at over 85mph on a side-valve, single gear, belt-drive 490cc Norton and at 70mph on a 249cc two-stroke Velocette.

Judd had been entered in the BMCRC race meeting on 29 March 1921. Appearing in the race programme that day was an announcement that a sponsor had put up three cups, 'to the total value of thirty guineas', one for each class, for the first club member to cover the flying kilometre at a speed of at least 80mph in Class B (350cc), 90mph in Class C (500cc), and 100mph in Class E (1000cc).

In this picture Judd had just covered the flying start kilometre at 92.44mph on this O'Donovan prepared Norton to win the Godfrey Cup for machines up to 500cc. The Norton has now acquired all-chain drive, including a clutch and gearbox, for the first time.

H R DAVIES   348cc AJS   21 May 1921

Late in 1920, during the traditional end of season record attempts session, Howard Davies cleared up the short-distance Class B (350cc solo) and Class F (350cc sidecar) records on his 348cc AJS racer.

On 19 October, he set a new Class B British one-way flying start kilometre record at 80.47 mph to win the Godfrey Cup, presented by Godfrey Ltd. for the first rider of a 350cc solo officially to exceed 80mph.

Under new FICM regulations for international records, for the flying start kilometre and the flying start mile only, the times would be the mean of two consecutive runs in opposing directions and within ten minutes. Davies now added to his tally by taking these two records at 77.40 and 73.32 mph respectively. The next day he attacked Class F sidecar records, succeeding in taking the flying start five miles and standing start 10 miles at 57.77mph and 55.18mph.

In the picture Davies is seen on the TT AJS he raced in 1921 and which he had brought to the junior 350cc Brooklands TT race at the meeting on 21 May. It was one of the new ohv racers which were destined to win both the Junior and Senior TT races in the Isle of Man that year. It differed considerably from the 1920 model, having a much modified engine, a new frame, wedge tank and a 3-speed countershaft gearbox instead of the six-speed transmission used for the 1920 Junior TT.

In this twenty four lap 350cc race Davies took an immediate lead which he steadily increased until a tightening piston eventually brought him into his pit to retire.

In 1924 he was to found the company that would build Massey-designed motorcycles of advanced design, under his own initials, HRD.

BMCRC 500 Mile Race   2 July 1921

Early in the year the BMCRC had announced that a 500 mile race would take place on the first Saturday in July. It would be for all the major solo classes. A member of the club, A G Miller, had commissioned Sydney Garrett, a well known rider, and a jeweller and silversmith, to make a 200 guinea cup to go to the overall winner. There were other prizes for various class and team winners.

On the day, no fewer than sixty four machines were lined up at the massed start for the I85 lap race. They presented a colourful spectacle as the riders in each of the capacity classes wore different coloured smocks.

After 200 miles, the Middlesborough rider Freddie Dixon, in his very first Brooklands race, led the 1000cc class on his Harley-Davidson whilst Norris (346cc Ivy) and Kershaw (249cc New Imperial) led the two smallest classes.

At half distance Dixon's front tyre burst and he skidded the length of the measured kilometre on the Railway Straight before parting company with his machine. He recovered, rode in, had the wheel changed and continued. Bert Le Vack had meanwhile taken over the lead, but the long distance was taking a toll on the field.

After various alarms and excursions, described in more detail over the page, Le Vack came in the overall winner at 70.42mph, Dixon finally coming home, exhausted, in second place.

Perhaps the most amazing performances were in the 350 and 250cc classes, with the original leaders, Norris and Kershaw, taking class wins at speeds of 51.69 and 50.34mph respectively.

This picture taken during the race shows little of the drama, merely the vast expanse of the track as four of the many competitors pass under the bridge on the Byfleet Banking.

500 Mile Race: H Le VACK   998cc Indian   2 July 1921

In the picture across the page, Le Vack is resting in the pits during the race, having pushed his 998cc V-twin Indian all the way back from the Railway Straight with a flat rear tyre.

He had been leading the race overall at 45 laps and, during his long push back with his heavy machine, the lead was taken over first by Douglas Davidson, then by Freddie Dixon, both on Harley-Davidsons.

Now, with a big smile on his face and a thumbs-up, Le Vack rests whilst the tyre is changed and his fuel tank filled. A large sponge, an open tin of something and a cool drink is all he has time for, plus encouragement from one of his helpers and, with his back to us, American Billy Wells, the Indian team boss. Wells also holds a glass, of a more managerial shape.

Suitably refreshed, Le Vack was soon back in the race and quickly making up lost ground, then again challenging for the lead. But tyre trouble was again to dog him, his crew having to rush out to him in a sidecar with a spare wheel.

Eventually, ten minutes ahead of an exhausted Freddie Dixon, Le Vack took the chequered flag to win the race overall and so take home the magnificent 200 guinea Miller Cup.

In the inset picture below, tired out, he is greeted by his delighted wife, his attempt at a welcoming kiss being foiled by a combination of her hat brim and his furry head protection.

D R O'DONOVAN   490cc Norton sidecar   9 July 1921

O'Donovan had raced at Brooklands, always with Nortons, well before the outbreak of war in 1914. Even in 1915 he had still covered a flying start kilometre at 82.85 mph on a side-valve, belt-driven Norton.

O'Donovan is seen here having come second in a two lap sidecar race on 9 July 1921. He had started from scratch and finished close behind the winner, F Longman, driving a 500cc Ariel, who had a 1 minute, 22 seconds start.

The passenger is Rex Judd, who had recently joined O'Donovan as his protégé test rider. In the race, he would have been in a prone position in the streamlined sidecar body, which was built to O'Donovan's order by Vickers at their aircraft factory prominently located opposite the motor-cycle pits and the Fork Start enclosure.

Norton's famous 490cc BS and BRS machines were developed and tested by O'Donovan and Judd and sold to the public with the guarantee of having exceeded 75 and 70mph over the flying kilometre, and of lapping the track at over 70 and 65mph respectively. Actually, the engines were all tested first in O'Donovan's old belt-drive Norton, then fitted into the new machines to be sold, at the rate of about twenty five a month.

A sensible man, O'Donovan gave up solo racing when he became a father, concentrating then on development work, the many successes of Judd, Denly and Staniland on his 490cc and 588 cc Nortons being evidence of his genius.

Later he joined the Raleigh Company, where he designed the 500cc machine that performed so well in the hands of C J Williams.

E F REMINGTON   348cc Blackburne   8 October 1921

The single cylinder, overhead valve 348cc Blackburne engine made its first appearance, appropriately enough, in a Blackburne machine, at the opening BMCRC meeting of 1921. In the hands of the experienced Eric Remington it was an immediate success, winning the 350cc flying start kilometre speed trials at 73.63mph and the 350cc scratch race that followed.

Remington had cut his teeth at Brooklands before the 1914-18 war, first on a 986cc Matchless-JAP, then on a 986cc NUT-JAP, having big accidents on both (see page 58).

Following the resumption of racing at Brooklands after the war, Remington raced both this 350 and a big twin machine – an ohv Blackburne fitted with one carburettor per cylinder, probably the first time such an arrangement had been applied to a V-twin in this country.

He was a great believer in the theory that smoothly curved exhaust pipes increased gas velocity, as seen here on his 348cc Blackburne. He had just won the three-lap Class B scratch race during the 1921 BMCRC championship meeting in October, at a speed of 69.39mph.

HRH The Duke of York's 994cc Trump-Anzani   20 May 1922

On this Saturday, the Duke of York gave his patronage to the combined Essex Motor Club and BMCRC race meeting. The Essex MC looked after the car events and the BMCRC the three motorcycle races.

The Duke had entered his chauffeur, S E Wood, in the 600cc solo handicap, on a 349cc Douglas. After a good start, he had mechanical problems and finished out of the placings. For the senior handicap for 1000cc solo machines, Wood was riding the Duke's 994cc Trump-Anzani, seen here. He wears the royal colours of a scarlet jersey with blue stripes and sleeves. Before the start of the race, the Duke was introduced to each of the riders.

The three lap handicap was won by 18 year old Jimmy Hall, on a 748cc Trump-JAP. The high point of the race was Claude Temple's attempt on his big, 989cc Harley-Davidson to overcome his severe handicapping. He failed, but such was his speed that he set up a new 1000cc solo flying start lap record at 97.28mph. For his part, Wood fared no better on the royal Trump than he had done on the Douglas.

H MARTIN   1078cc Morgan-Anzani 10 June 1922

After the 1914-18 war, Harry Martin continued for a time to race motorcycles, using one of his own products, a 496cc Martin-MAG and, occasionally, a Matchless-MAG. Now, partly because of being nowadays referred to in the press reports as 'one of Brooklands' old stalwarts', Martin had decided to revert to his cyclecar days, simply solved by borrowing the works 1078cc Morgan-Anzani.

   Having taken third place with it in a 'passenger machine' scratch race in May 1922, he fancied his chances with the Morgan in the BMCRC's monthly meeting in June, this time winning the five lap handicap race at 70.58mph.

   On this occasion, the Anzani engine designer, Hubert Hagens, was on hand to keep an eye on things, especially as the Morgan was fitted with his very latest eight-valve racing engine.

   Each cylinder had a bore and stroke of 85mm by 95mm, and each head had two sparking plugs fired by its own double-spark magneto, whilst carburation was provided by a triple-venturi Zenith instrument.

Col R N STEWART   994cc Trump-Anzani 14 June 1922

One has to go back to 1911 to find the first reference to Bob Stewart, then just a lieutenant, turning out on an even then quite dated Trump-JAP. He continued using the side-valve engined machine with single gear belt-drive until, just before the war, he brought out a 349cc twin-cylinder NSU to set up a new nine hour Class B (350cc solo) record to settle a bet with fellow officers in his regiment.

Returning to the track after the war, now a full colonel, he dusted off his ancient belt-driven 4hp Trump to win a solo handicap in July 1921. For his next appearance in early May 1922, Col. Stewart's old Trump now sported, remarkably,

one of Hubert Hagen's 994cc Anzani V-twin engines, also entering it later in May in the meeting described on a previous page at which the Duke of York was introduced to all the riders, including Col. Stewart, of course.

The high point of his year, however, was here, on 14 June, when he attacked Class E (1000cc) records from two to five hours with his Trump-Anzani, now chain-driven. Due to mechanical problems, he was unable to continue beyond the first two hours, but still took that one record at a speed of 78.85mph. As ever, the designer of the Anzani engine, Hubert Hagens, was on hand with his congratulations.

C G PULLIN 346cc Douglas sidecar 17 June 1922

Greatly impressed by Cyril Pullin's tuning skill as amply demonstrated on a big Zenith-Anzani, Les Bailey of the Douglas concern – and Pullin's future brother-in-law – persuaded him to try his hand on a Douglas.

Following a number of impressive race and record breaking successes with Douglas machines, including becoming the first officially to do 100mph on a 500cc motorcycle, he was entered in the 200 mile sidecar races on 17 June 1922, organized by the Ealing and District MCC. The three separate scratch races, for 350, 600 and 1000cc outfits, were to be run concurrently. Each class was identified by the sidecars being painted blue, red and yellow respectively.

Pullin, on a 346cc Douglas outfit, built up an early lead and increased it steadily to win his class easily at 51.78mph. He was later reported as saying that his throttle was set only half open for most of the 200 mile, 74 lap race.

In the main picture, Pullin, number 14, is seen overtaking H Robinson's 345cc Wooler sidecar. The skids which now had to be fitted in case of the sidecar wheel coming off can be clearly seen. Below, Pullin is being congratulated after the race, with Les Bailey's hand on his shoulder. His passenger, after four hours of discomfort in the sidecar, does not yet feel like joining in the fun.

A G FENN   739cc Martinsyde sidecar   17 June 1922

On the previous page we saw that the 350cc class in the Ealing and District Club's 200 mile sidecar race was won by Cyril Pullin on his Douglas outfit. The 1000cc sidecar race being run at the same time revealed some interesting innovations, including Freddie Dixon's 989cc Harley-Davidson outfit, which had the sidecar wheel driven as well, by chain connected to the engine by a countershaft.

Even more unusual was the Martinsyde combination of Archie Fenn, seen here in the background, towards the grandstand, making a good start. In this case, the sidecar was fitted on the off-side, and had a flexible chassis similar to those used in America. The third wheel was mounted in a forked bracket designed to lean over on bends, the movement being controlled by a tie rod attached to the rear fork member some six inches above the wheel spindle.

Inside the sidecar body Fenn had arranged a seven gallon fuel tank with pressure feed to the main tank, and two charged oil guns.

Soon after his excellent start he had to pull in with clutch slip, losing 35 minutes to repairs. When he got going again his speed was most encouraging, but to no avail as, on his fiftieth lap, he had to retire when the rear wheel chain sprocket sheared off the hub.

The race was won by Douglas Davidson's rather more conventional 998cc Indian outfit, followed in second place by the ever-present Bert Le Vack on a 998cc Zenith-JAP.

R WEATHERELL   349cc Weatherell-Blackburne   15 July 1922

The main event of the BMCRC members' meeting on 15 July 1922 was the 100 mile, 37 lap Mellano Cup handicap. For this big race an experimental handicap based on distance rather than time was to be tried. The principle was that riders were to be stationed at various distances from the Fork, and starting on a signal given by a marshal alongside.

The race was run at a stiff pace from the beginning, so much so that the field of forty-two starters was being steadily thinned out due to various problems, such as from sparking-plugs and, particularly, rear tyres.

The final result was a convincing win, at 66.04mph, for Reg Weatherell riding his 349cc Weatherell-Blackburne, a machine that he had built himself. He is seen here being hoisted by frightfully enthusiastic supporters, in celebration of his very first win on his own creation.

Even before this 100 mile race took place, there had been a new build-up of opposition from the local residents, particularly, it was claimed, due to the noise from long motorcycle races such as the 1921 500 mile event and the more recent 200 mile sidecar races in June.

Accordingly, a notice had already been issued before the 15 July meeting by the Clerk of the Course, Col Lindsay Lloyd, that all vehicles using the track, especially motorcycles, must be adequately silenced on pain of being banned from the whole Brooklands estate. This would, it said, come into effect immediately.

Despite this a number of entrants at the meeting seemed unaware of the new regulation and some open exhausts had to receive some emergency treatment on the spot.

V E HORSMAN   490cc Norton   21 October 1922

Victor Horsman was one of the top tuner-riders of the vintage years in particular, winning races and breaking records, first on Norton and then on Triumph machines.

On 9 September 1920, Emerson, riding the latest version of the already highly developed 398cc ABC had covered 70.46miles in the hour. Two days later, at the sixth BMCRC meeting, Horsman on his side-valve, single-gear, belt-drive Norton raised this to 71.68mph, a good start to a decade of successful racing.

Here, two years later, Horsman, now with overhead valves, gearbox and all-chain drive, had won the 500cc solo race at 81.35mph, during which he set a new flying start 5 mile record of 89.25mph. In the day's 600cc sidecar race, he also triumphed with a win and the same record for Class F of 73.55mph.

Between1920 and 1927, Horsman was to win ten championship races. It was believed that most of the quickest men in these events were now using alcohol-based fuels.

H Le VACK 980cc Zenith-JAP 27 October 1922

In 1922, Le Vack joined J A Prestwich and Sons, the makers of JAP engines, in their experimental and racing department.

He appeared on this Zenith on 8 April 1922, finishing second to Temple's Harley-Davidson in two solo races. There were, probably, two of these big Zeniths, the other one being used only for sidecar racing. It is fairly certain that it was on that machine that Le Vack took second place behind Douglas Davidson's Indian in the 1000cc 200 mile sidecar race on 17 June 1922, the event described on page 110.

However, it was on the Zenith seen here that

Le Vack made history that year when, on a cold October day, in intermittent drizzle, he covered five miles from a flying start in two minutes 59.48 seconds, a speed of 100.29mph. This was the first time that a British motorcycle rider had established an international record at over 100mph, and the first time that a motorcycle had lapped Brooklands at over 100mph.

Four days later, he established a new world's record for the flying-start kilometre with a mean speed of 102.9mph, and, on 18 November, set a new record for the classic hour distance, when he covered 89 miles 1519 yards.

I P RIDDOCH   994cc Zenith-Blackburne   14 April 1923

In 1920, when Ian Riddoch was at Oxford, his tutor, L P Openshaw, owned one of the very rare 500cc V-twin Zenith-JAPs and a 986cc Zenith-JAP and sidecar, both of which he used at Brooklands and in speed trials. Later, when the University authorities ruled that undergraduates only were allowed to compete in such activities, Riddoch bought both machines and used them at Brooklands.

In 1921, he approached the Blackburne and Zenith companies to build him two machines incorporating the big V-twin Blackburne engines in Zenith loop frames, one for solo racing, the other for sidecar events. On 29 July 1922, at the Clipstone speed trials, Riddoch became the first motorcyclist to exceed 100mph on a public road, being timed at 101.12mph over the flying start half mile.

In the picture he has either just won, or is just about to win the 1000cc one lap race at the Public Schools MCC meeting on 14 April 1923. The Blackburne engine is now fitted with two carburettors and two magnetos, the second of which is fitted above the gearbox. By the look of the blurred magneto chains, the engine appears to be running. One wonders if the slashed exhaust pipe ends would have met the new 'adequately silenced' regulations.

T G MEETEN   147cc Francis-Barnet-Villiers   14 July 1923

At the Motor Cycling Club's race meeting on Saturday 14 July 1923, Claude Temple now had his 996cc British Anzani going well after an indifferent start to the season.

However, in the five lap championship solo handicap race at this meeting, Temple, on scratch, had to concede no less than eleven and a half minutes to the limit man Tommy Meeten, whose little two-stroke machine was on its fourth lap by the time that Temple was flagged away. For all that, Temple snatched second place,

setting new Class E (1000cc solo) flying start five mile and standing start ten mile records at 104.31 and 101.51mph respectively. Meeten had also won the first race of the meeting, a three lap 350cc solo handicap, at 40.46mph.

For the next six years, Meeten kept faith with his lightweight machine, moving up to Class 6, (l75cc solo), with a Villiers l72cc two-stroke engine, with which he continued to set long distance and speed records. Later, in 1929, he raced the same machine with a sidecar.

C W JOHNSTON 248cc Cotton-Blackburne 21 July 1923

The 200 mile sidecar races organised in 1922 by the enterprising Ealing and District MCC had been so successful that the BMCRC had decided that their July meeting in 1923 would consist of four 200 mile races for all solo classes.

On the day, the first of the races was for Class A machines, that is up to 250cc. The 73 lap race was run at a cracking pace which put paid to seven of the eleven starters well before the end of the race.

On lap 49, Paddy Johnston on his Cotton-Blackburne had taken the lead and he was to hold it to the end, finishing at an average speed of 58.38mph. He is seen here after the race, with his two helpers in numbered skull caps.

Johnston's ability on the track was liable to be overlooked due to the publicity given to his road-racing successes. He always raced Blackburne-engined motorcycles, for a time later in 1923 with a 592cc V-twin OEC Blackburne sidecar outfit. With this he came second to Victor Horsman on his new 599cc Triumph sidecar at the BMCRC meeting in October. As we shall see later in our story, he was to bring out the OEC machine again, this time in solo form, early in 1924.

Johnston returned to the Cotton-Blackburne formula a year later and finally, with a 498cc Blackburne unit installed, earned his 100mph lap Gold Star in March 1929.

A DENLY   490cc Norton   21 July 1923

Norton's racing manager, D R O'Donovan, was facing the 1923 season without a rider following Rex Judd's decision to join the Douglas concern.

His problem was solved in an extraordinary way. Whilst out one day in Weybridge he was nearly in collision with a butcher's delivery boy riding an old 1917 350cc side-valve Douglas with great verve. The lad's name was Albert Denly. Impressed with the youngster's handling of his machine through the village, O'Donovan asked him to come to the track and show what he could do on one of the works Nortons.

So good was Denly that within two months of joining O'Donovan he had set a new 500cc hour record at 82.66mph. Pleased with Denly's natural ability and eagerness to learn O'Donovan nominated him to ride the works Norton in that year's 200 mile solo race.

However, Denly being of such small stature, a virtually new machine had to be built to suit him. More of a problem was his light weight: the minimum requirement for riders in the race was nine stone six pounds. O'Donovan overcame this with lead sheet screwed to the soles of Denly's boots and more lead sewn into a floral cushion tied to his waist with cord.   The plans were crowned with success, Denly winning the 500cc race at a speed of 77.01mph.

On the right he is seen at a pit stop in the race, taking a drink in the background whilst his Norton is refuelled. The lead-weighted cushion is very prominent. O'Donovan himself, in the skull cap, is supervising the refuelling and looking quite pleased with how things were going.

Denly's cushion can be seen more clearly in the post-race picture below, as can the edge of the lead sheet sole on his boot.

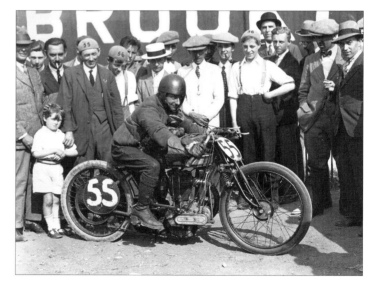

H Le VACK   344cc New Imperial-JAP   21 July 1923

We have already seen in the previous two stories that, in the BMCRC 200 mile solo race meeting in July 1923, the 250cc event was won by Paddy Johnston and the 500cc race by O'Donovan's novice works rider, Bert Denly.

This left the 350 and 1000cc races to be settled and it was none other than Bert Le Vack who brought off a remarkable double by winning both 200 mile races in the one day. In the morning, in spite of some plug and tyre trouble, he won the 350cc race at 72.66mph on the New Imperial-JAP seen here. Standing with him are his pit attendants. The one with refreshment in hand is Sid Moram, his one-time business associate but, by now, employed with Le Vack at the JAP engine factory.

In the main picture on the right, Le Vack is being chaired by admirers having achieved his second victory of the day, this time in the 1000cc class, riding his 996cc Brough Superior. In the centre is Moram, to whom was to go a great deal of the credit for this unique double achievement. For, whilst Le Vack was fully occupied with the 350cc New Imperial, Moram, with the assistance of the un-named mechanic seen in both pictures, built the Brough in the three days preceding the race. Then, after only three practice laps on the machine, Le Vack won the race in faultless style, at 83.34mph.

F W DIXON   989cc Harley-Davidson sidecar   22 September 1923

This is the big Harley outfit that Freddie Dixon raced during 1923. Here, at the BMCRC race meeting on 22 September, Dixon had been duelling for the lead in the 1000cc sidecar scratch race with Bert Le Vack's Brough. Dixon actually led off the Byfleet Banking on the last lap, but Le Vack snatched the win at 80.72mph. Although the sidecar passenger is here facing the camera, for the race he would have been lying prone, with his head facing to the rear.

Freddie Dixon was one of the few men who was able to handle the fearsome loop-framed, eight-valve V-twin Harleys. He won many races with them, especially in solo form, such as at the October BMCRC meeting, when Dixon had his solo 998cc Harley really going, winning the 1000cc race at 100.10mph.

Whilst Dixon continued to campaign Harley-Davidsons in both solo and sidecar forms, he also raced solo versions of Douglas, Zenith and, occasionally, Brough Superior machines in the late 1920's. Thereafter, he had many successful years racing cars at Brooklands, especially the Rileys he prepared himself.

W D MARCHANT   348cc Chater-Lea   23 March 1924

Nobody really knows who was the very first motorcyclist to ride on the then new Brooklands motor course. One story has it that some naval officers came up to the track late in 1907 and circulated until their engines became red hot. Another, rather charming legend has it that the eleven year Dougal Marchant, who would in the future become famous there, pedalled round on his mother's tricycle even before the course was officially opened.

Be that as it may, Marchant had gained some valuable experience at Brooklands from early in 1921, riding Motosacoche, Sheffield-Henderson and Zenith machines. But it was with Chater-Lea that, from late 1923 onwards, he began to establish himself as one of the most outstanding exponents of motorcycle engineering and design. He also rode competitively with great success.

The ohv Blackburne-engined motorcycle in the inset picture alongside was probably built from scratch by Marchant. Dating from late 1923, it was used only for record-breaking when it would bear the name of the firm engaging Marchant for that particular purpose.

In the main picture he is on his first Chater-Lea, having won the 350cc three lap scratch race at the first BMCRC meeting of 1924, at a speed of just over 82mph. A few days later, on 1 April, Marchant was timed in one direction over the flying start kilometre at 100.81mph, thereby becoming the first rider of a '350' to exceed 100mph at Brooklands.

The engine is invariably referred to as being an experimental overhead-camshaft Blackburne. Others are convinced that, although some Blackburne parts may have been used, it was designed and built by Marchant himself.

C W JOHNSTON   592cc OEC-Blackburne   19 April 1924

As we have said before, Johnston always raced Blackburne-engined motorcycles. Here he is on something of a rarity, an OEC machine fitted with a 592cc V-twin Blackburne engine. Despite a high wind, Johnston had won the three lap solo handicap race, at 85.57mph, during the BMCRC meeting on 19 April 1924. A handsome machine indeed which, with open exhausts, must have sounded good as well.

But not in the opinion of the local residents, who had already brought heavy pressure to bear on the Brooklands authorities to reduce the noise of engines or risk the revival of the injunction already threatened the previous year.

Following further tightening of the existing silencing regulations, the BMCRC members in particular felt that they were being victimised, especially when Dougal Marchant was refused admission to the track on account of the alleged noisiness of his machines. The picture on the previous page is worth another look!

Regular riders threatened to boycott the forthcoming meeting of the club on 10 May, and, after a meeting, resolved by twenty-three votes to three to abstain from riding in the afternoon races. A resolution was passed objecting to the proposed restrictions and pointing to the fees, rents and other revenues paid by the members to the Brooklands authorities.

The eventual outcome of the riders' strike was inevitably a compromise, especially in view of the undertaking given to the disgruntled local residents by the BARC that noisy vehicles would be prohibited from using the track.

The existing, somewhat vague silencing rules were now supplemented by a new and detailed silencer specification, and it was made clear that, with effect from Saturday 24 May 1924, any machine not meeting the new regulations would not be allowed on the Brooklands estate.

H Le VACK   245cc New Imperial-JAP   7 June 1924

On this is page we have a demonstration of Le Vack's professional and dedicated approach to his career as a motorcycle engineer/rider.

Here he is at the BMCRC meeting on 7 June 1924 with a dohc 245cc New Imperial-JAP, the engine being one of the first ever fitted with a twin exhaust port cylinder head. In the first race of the day, a three lap 250cc solo scratch race, he came home the winner at the remarkable speed of 82.18 mph. For his second win of the day, a similar three-lapper for 350cc machines, Le Vack had switched to a 344cc New Imperial.

Of the four one lap sprint races that followed, Le Vack won two of them, the 350 and 500cc solo races at 81.37 and 84.13mph respectively, still riding the 344cc double overhead camshaft New Imperial-JAP.

He rounded off his day by winning the 1000cc solo race at a speed of 94.50mph, this time on his trusty 996cc Brough Superior-JAP, which he just happened to have with him at the time.

It is interesting if somewhat pedantic to stress that Le Vack's 245cc JAP was not the first ever twin exhaust port engine. W D Chitty (see page 28) raced a 482cc Frays-JAP with one exhaust valve and two exhaust ports as early as 1910.

J S WRIGHT   344cc Zenith-JAP   7 June 1924

On Saturday 8 September 1923, the Public Schools MCC organised a motorcycle race meeting at Brooklands, in conjunction with the City and Guilds Engineering College MCC. Held in brilliant sunshine, the programme was made up of a series of one and two lap scratch and handicap races and an all-class handicap over three laps.

The only known name which made it into the press report of the event was to be that of Nigel Spring, on a 490cc ohv Norton, whom we will feature in these pages in due course. Also there, it appears, riding a 249cc side-valve Zenith-JAP, was one Joe Wright who was to win his first ever race at the meeting.

In the fullness of time to become one of the most famous of Brooklands riders, Wright was first noticed, albeit 'as a relatively unknown rider', having won a race at the same BMCRC meeting in June 1924 at which Bert Le Vack scored heavily, as related on the previous page. Wright would no doubt have liked to have had one of the 344cc dohc engines that Le Vack was using.

But something about Wright's machine was unusual. This was the exhaust expansion box beneath the gearbox, which earned favourable comments, particularly from the scrutineers, in the light of the recently introduced silencing regulations which were now being strictly enforced, as we have already seen.

C S STANILAND   490cc Norton   7 June 1924

Coincidentally another 'newcomer' rider at the BMCRC fourth meeting of 1924 at which Joe Wright first appeared was similarly destined to become a household name in Brooklands circles, firstly on motorcycles, then in racing cars.

This was Chris Staniland, who won the 500cc three lap handicap race at 76.27mph, Wright having won the 350cc event earlier in the day. Both mens' pleasure at their wins must have been later somewhat dampened having read

In the press reports that these races were judged as being 'very tame affairs'.

Whereas Wright was to go on to specialise in racing big machines, mostly in Class E (1000cc), Staniland would make his name on both solos and sidecars, in the 250, 350 and 500cc classes. At first he rode Nortons such as this one for O'Donovan and Spring and later on, Excelsior machines under the management of the ace tuner and rider, J S 'Woolley' Worters.

C TEMPLE   996cc Montgomery-British Anzani   7 June 1924

Claude Temple's first appearance in a race at Brooklands was at the Motor Cycling Club's first post-war meeting in July 1920. He came second in a 1000cc solo scratch race riding a 989cc Harley-Davidson. In the next nine years of the vintage period, Temple was never to ride anything other than big V-twin machines.

He is now seen here at the same meeting as on the previous two pages, astride his massive 996cc Montgomery-British Anzani, having won a five lap 1000cc solo scratch race at 105.32mph, the highest speed to that date for a motorcycle race at Brooklands. Temple has used a Harley-Davidson frame and front forks for this special machine, fitted with a 57 degree ohc V-twin engine, the brainchild of Belgian engine designer Hubert Hagens, seen standing, fag in hand as always, behind Temple's machine.

This dramatic-looking motorcycle was to be developed by Temple over several years, the name changing from time to time depending upon the company or individual having an interest, usually promotional, in the machine.

It is interesting to note that Joe Wright, who was making a rather more modest contribution to the day's proceedings, would in due course emerge as Claude Temple's main competition in the big machine class. Indeed, eventually, the two would end up as partners in the business of world records.

A DENLY 490cc Norton 7 June 1924

During his four years close association with O'Donovan, Bert Denly won the 1923 Class C (500cc) 200 miles solo race, as recounted on page 126, the 1926 championship race and the one hour record on four separate occasions, all in the same class. His winning speed on the Norton in the championship race was 95.59mph, and his fastest lap of that year was 99.01mph.

Between these major successes, O'Donovan entered Denly in a number of club events in the interests of development and, of course, further exposure of the Norton name. Thus, at the same BMCRC meeting in 1924 that Staniland and Wright first made their mark and Le Vack and Temple were winning as usual, Denly in turn won the 500cc three lap scratch race at 85.37mph.

However, all the talk in the Paddock was still about the stringent new silencer regulations, which is why Joe Wright's intriguing expansion chamber had caused something of a flutter.

So did the curious swelling on Bert Denly's exhaust. This ingenious device had been designed by Cyril Pullin, the Douglas specialist, and it worked on the principle of the exhaust gases entering tangentially and leaving centrally. It was claimed to give only one per cent loss of efficiency as against the five per cent loss with the normal type.

Efficient the device may have been, but whether or not it also met the new specifications as regards noise reduction is not mentioned in the press reports.

The Pond Start Public Enclosure 1924

A rare picture of the Fork, or Pond Start public enclosure on a BMCRC members' day, mostly taken up by parked motorcycles. The entrance to the enclosure would have been off Weybridge Road to the south of the ordinary entrance for the public's motor cars.

In the period after the 1914-18 war, motorcycle race meetings at Brooklands seldom drew large crowds. Instead they attracted the same few hundreds of devoted enthusiasts, for the most part highly informed on technical matters and who was now riding what machine.

Between competitors and spectators there existed a peculiar affinity which was never even approached in the sphere of motor racing at the track. At the same time it was not unusual to find leading racing drivers amongst the spectators at these meetings: many of them, after all, had started their days at Brooklands on two or three wheels, Malcolm Campbell, W O Bentley, Chris Staniland, Freddie Dixon, Tony Vandervell, Frank Halford, Pat Driscoll and Kaye Don, amongst others.

The picture also shows that bookmakers, permanently located for all meetings ever since the track opened in the main public enclosure near to the results board, also set up their boards for motorcycle races starting at the Fork. It is just possible to make out the names chalked up so far by bookie Bill Collins: Temple, Dixon, Baldwin, Koehler, Glover, Parker, Longman and C W Johnston, although without the odds.

Unusually for a photograph from the Hartley archive, the event is neither identified nor dated. There is just the clue '1923/24'. Paddy Johnston was usually riding his quarter-litre Cotton-Blackburne, suggesting, perhaps, an experts handicap or suchlike: all the others rode 500, 750 or 1000cc machines.

It is difficult to decide in which of the two years the event took place. It is just possible that it was in the late summer of 1923. More likely that it was between March and mid-June 1924, because it was in March that year that Tommy Koehler first appeared at the track on a 988cc Zenith-JAP. After a number of successes in 1000cc class races, he entered a small, inter-club meeting on Saturday 14 June, winning the two lap experts' unlimited scratch race, at a speed of 86.62mph.

Unhappily, the following Saturday, it appears that, in nearby Kingston-upon-Thames, he was killed in a road accident when his motorcycle was in collision with a lorry.

C W G LACEY   344cc Cotton-JAP   23 July 1924

Bill Lacey had started his Brooklands career in May 1922, barely turned twenty years old, on a 499cc Rudge, coming eighth in a scratch race for motorcycles up to 500cc.

He would have to wait for a couple of years before he began to attract attention, now racing a Cotton-JAP, with a second place in a 350cc handicap race at the Surbiton Motor Club's meeting on 19 July 1924. Only four days later, at the Essex Motor Club's annual meeting, Lacey scored his first win, in the 500cc junior handicap at a cracking speed of 81.91 mph.

The picture shows Lacey after his win, the Cotton looking as if it had just come from the Motor Cycle Show. On the right, with his hand on Lacey's shoulder, is Mr Lacey Snr. His son's most ardent supporter, he was always to be seen on hand whenever and wherever young Bill was racing or record-breaking.

Looking over Mr Lacey's right shoulder is Ted Baragwanath, a real character, who rode big V-twin sidecar outfits. He is easily recognised by the stiff wing-collar he always wore, even when he was racing.

Although something of a digression, an incident during the earlier meeting which Bill Lacey had taken part in is worth recalling, if only as an example of the determination of some outer circuit riders.

According to the race report of the day, during the other motorcycle race included in the programme of this car meeting 'M A McEvoy (996cc McEvoy-Anzani) brought spectators' hearts to their mouths with a series of terrifying wobbles all down the straight past the stands. He repeated the performance on lap three, but managed to stay aboard his big machine.

'It transpired later that he had torn off his gear change lever with a fierce change at the start and was now steering with one hand, and holding his gear in with the other, for the rest of the race.'

Not surprisingly, McEvoy does not appear to figure amongst the three top finishers.

T R ALLCHIN   996cc Zenith-JAP   23 July 1924

Also entered in the Essex Motor Club's annual meeting at which Lacey had scored his first win was Tommy Allchin, riding a very interesting 996cc Zenith-JAP. The engine was one of the few 80 x 99mm four-cam, side-valve, long-stroke JAP V-twins first used by Le Vack in his Zenith during 1922. This engine was never put into production. Apart from the engine, Allchin's machine was le Vack's 1923 works Zenith.

The Essex MC's meeting was somewhat down on entries due to several big events falling on the same day. The club had also been obliged to hold the meeting on a Wednesday because the track was fully booked up on Saturdays throughout the summer.

It was therefore particularly easy for Allchin to win the three lap 1000cc senior handicap at 98.62mph. Of his many successes at the track, his win on a works 996cc Zenith-JAP in the 1000cc class of the 1924 200 miles solo races the following September, was undoubtedly the most outstanding. He won at 87.38mph and, in so doing, broke the two hour record.

The following week, Allchin was riding as passenger with E B Ware who had entered his Morgan-JAP in the Junior Car Club's 200 mile race for cars. During the race the Morgan crashed heavily at 90mph due to a mechanical failure. Both men were thrown out on to the track, Ware being badly hurt. Allchin escaped comparatively lightly.

Returning to the subject of his Zenith, it is interesting to note that it was actually very few riders who regularly competed at Brooklands on big-twin machines, whatever make.

Generally speaking, they tended to be somewhat temperamental and less efficient, especially over long distances, than the single cylindered machines. Most riders disliked them for their weight, indifferent performance for their capacity, and discomfort. Some riders even admitted to being scared of them.

R M N SPRING   490cc Norton   2 August 1924

All the big names had turned out for the BMCRC's sixth members' meeting of 1924, Marchant, Horsman, Denly, Judd, Temple, Allchin and Baldwin, amongst others. The ten-race entry list read like a Who's Who of the vintage period at Brooklands.

Amongst the field was Nigel Spring, on a 490cc Norton, who won the 500cc three lap handicap race at 83.84mph. Over time he enjoyed a string of successes as a Norton rider, but it was in the field of management that his name would become a by-word.

In the later stages of his riding career he had participated in long-distance records for Norton such as the Double Twelve and 24 hours, with others being brought in to share the riding, one of whom was Bert Denly, at that time O'Donovan's main works rider.

Having later turned his attention to tuning rather than racing, Spring inevitably became more closely involved with O'Donovan, with the result that, in early 1927, he took over the management of Norton's development and racing programme when O'Donovan retired.

Not long after, Spring was approached by the Stevens brothers, who made him a handsome offer to manage the AJS racing team. William Mansell, the head of Norton Motors, was to realise that this was an offer that Spring could not refuse and the two parted on good terms.

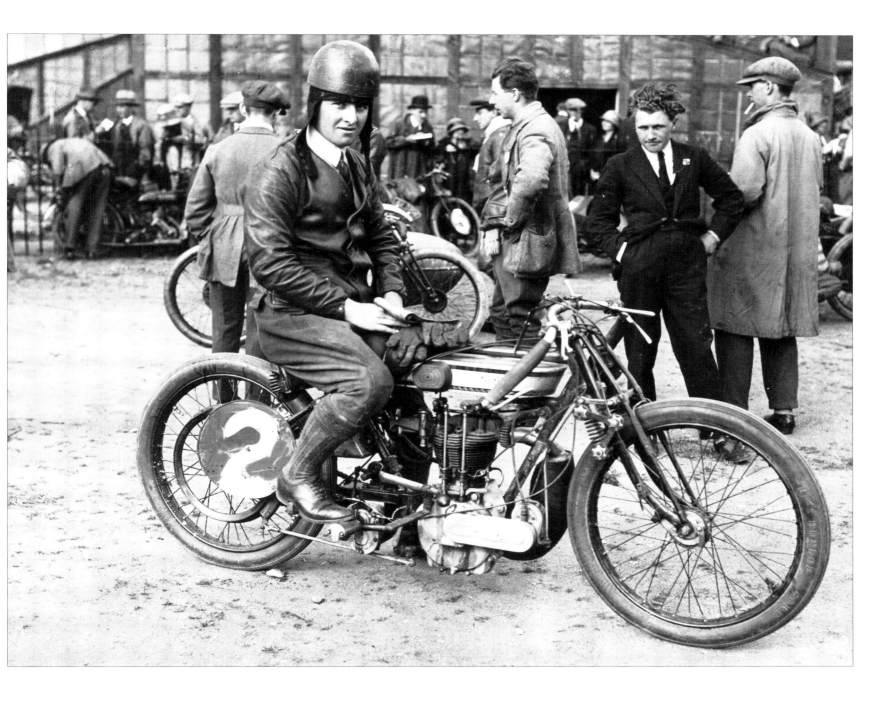

R E HUMPHRIES   989cc Harley-Davidson sidecar   23 August 1924

Humphries announced his arrival on the scene at Brooklands in a dramatic manner by not only entering the 1923 BMCRC 200 mile solo race on a 994cc V-twin Indian, but actually bringing the difficult machine home in third place behind Bert Le Vack and Freddie Dixon.

He had so clearly enjoyed himself that he appeared the following month in the Ealing Club's 200 mile sidecar races. Towards the end of the 1000cc race, he had to pull the Indian to the side of the track with the carburettor on fire, a common Indian problem. A Pyrene extinguisher attendant was quickly on the scene and the flames put out, but he could not continue.

For 1924, he had swopped the Indian for a Harley-Davidson outfit and is seen here having won the 1000cc class in the 200 mile sidecar races, again organised by the Ealing and District MCC. During the race, Le Vack, Dixon, Temple and Allchin all had problems, leaving Humphries the comfortable winner at 69.66mph.

The only problem Humphries and his 'British Warm' overcoated passenger appear to have encountered was the breaking up of the sidecar body due to the rough Brooklands surface, a not uncommon occurance; hence the strap.

R T GROGAN 490cc Norton 6 September 1924

Grogan was one of the Norton private owners competing at Brooklands, firstly on a side-valve model 16H and later, on an ohv model 18. On that machine he had won the 1000cc three lap handicap race in August 1923 at a speed of 80.90mph.

Grogan's best win came in a long distance race. Here, on 6 September 1924, on one of O'Donovan's works Nortons, he had just won the 200 mile 500cc solo race at 79.81mph, a new Class C record for the distance.

O'Donovan had entered another of his Nortons in the race, ridden by the previous year's race winner Bert Denly, but he failed to finish. So O'Donovan was well pleased with Grogan, who appears oil-soaked but with tie still in place.

In 1927, Grogan was invited by R M N Spring to ride his 588cc Norton in that year's 200 mile solo race in Class E (1000cc). At half distance, Grogan was some three miles in the lead and averaging nearly 93mph. However, when accelerating away after a refuelling pit stop, he skidded on the rain-soaked track into a post and was forced to retire.

The Brighton Speed Trials   6 September 1924

On the same Saturday that Grogan was winning the Class C race in the BMCRC's classic 200 mile race meeting, down at the seaside other Brooklands motorcycle riders were trying out their machines at Brighton's annual Speed Trials.

Here, from a standing start, competitors would run in pairs up the straight half-mile course, each being individually and accurately timed. These all-out acceleration trials were regularly made use of by the likes of Fernihough, Pope, Beart and the Bickell brothers, amongst other Brooklands notables.

In 1905, the great Brightonian, Sir Harry Preston, was successful in persuading the town council to lay a motor racing track, a tarmac surfaced road and the first of its kind, along the Brighton sea front from the Palace Pier to within a quarter of a mile of Black Rock.

It was then named the Madeira Road and was the venue of the first Brighton Speed Trials in 1905. The Madeira Terrace, the elevated walk running along the sea front above the road, now named the Madeira Drive, made a splendid grandstand and, in Sir Harry's words, "thousands of people watched the races from here, and all Brighton and half England talked of nothing else during that exciting week."

The Brighton Speed Trials have run each year ever since to this day, punctuated only by the two world wars.

In the picture, actually taken at the 1924 event, two sidecar outfits are about to get the time-honoured push start, watched by an enormous crowd. That day the fastest time of the day was by Brooklands rider Eric Spencer on his solo 499cc Douglas in 26 seconds, an average speed of 69.2 mph. The fastest car, a 1496cc AC, recorded 28 seconds, at 64.2mph.

H M WALTERS 344cc Jappic 21 March 1925

This 4-wheel cyclecar made its first appearance, but did not compete, at this, the BMCRC's first meeting of 1925. Designed by H M Walters, a regular motorcycle competitor on Zenith-JAPs, and Vivian Prestwich of the JAP engine concern, its diminutive size and attractive appearance received a very favourable reception.

The frame was of ash with steel flitch-plates, with tubular cross-members. The two-port, 344cc JAP racing engine was mounted vertically some two feet behind the front axle, driving by chain to a three-speed gearbox mounted on a cross-member. The final drive was by chain to the open axle which was suspended on reversed quarter-elliptic rear springs. The tubular front axle was carried on two underslung quarter-elliptic springs, each with its own shock absorber.

The beautifully crafted cockpit could just about accommodate two people but as the final chain drive passed between them it was seldom used as a two-seater! A padded sleeve for the right arm was recommended for the driver.

The Jappic was registered for the road and there was talk of others being made for sale, but nothing came of this. Weighing under 4 cwt, the machine allowed Walters to post all new four-wheel cyclecar records from both standing and flying starts, at speeds of up to 70 mph.

Douglas Hawkes later took records with it at Montlhery in France, with 350 and 500cc JAP engines, until, sadly, it was to be lost in the fire which destroyed his workshops there.

J EMERSON   994cc Zenith-Blackburne   25 April 1925

After an absence from Brooklands for a while, Jack Emerson turned up at an ACU race meeting in late April 1925 on Ian Riddoch's 994cc Zenith-Blackburne, giving him victory in the three lap 350 – 1000cc solo handicap at 100.4lmph.

For some time now, Riddoch had felt that his big machine was out of date. He had come to the view that research into motorcycle racing would be more productive by concentrating on smaller engines, extracting more power by such means as supercharging and special fuels, by now becoming a widely held viewpoint.

After the 1914-18 war, the increase in speeds in motorcycle races began to show a marked difference between the large and small engine capacities. Whereas the big V-twins improved slowly, the speeds of the smaller machines rose in a spectacular fashion.

Profiting by Ricardo's research, people began to experiment with much higher compression ratios in small bore cylinders which, together with newly developed alcohol fuels, soon allowed compression ratios as high as nine to one, as against the five to one of the big engines.

By such means it became a much more rewarding business to go record breaking in the small classes than in the larger. So there began the same pursuit of higher power output from lesser cylinder capacity as was already happening in car racing , but arising from quite a different motive. This was the issue of race win and record bonus payments which tended to determine, to a greater or lesser extent, the outcome of a race.

One story, reportedly true, tells of an overheard conversation in the gents' toilets at Brooklands between three crack riders who, in the belief that they were alone, agreed to carve up the afternoon's races between them. This worked out so well that five out of the seven races panned out as they had agreed. As far as the crowd were concerned, they left the track convinced that they had witnessed the finest day's racing for many a month.

A similar, but much more common practice, was the arrangement amongst the quickest riders in respect to record bonus payments, a much more fruitful source of income than race winnings. It was a simple matter of taking it in turns to break records, ideally by just the minimum improvement required, so as to leave room for whoever's turn it was to claim the next month's bonus; and so on.

Most of this record activity was kept for the Autumn, as it interfered less with racing and coincided with the annual Motor Cycle Show, when sponsors liked to have something to boast about.

J W WHEELER   494cc Douglas   9 May 1925

The first BMCRC race meeting of 1925, on 21 March, was the first motorcycle meeting to be run under the new silencing regulations introduced as a result of yet further complaints from irate local residents.

The rules had been further tightened up over the winter lay-off, a new clause requiring the fitting of fish-tail silencer ends of specified dimensions. The riders had accepted the new regulations as inevitable if motorcycle racing was to continue at the track.

One of the newcomers signed up for the club's 1925 programme of events was the amateur J W Wheeler on his 494cc Douglas. His very first race at the March meeting was a three lap 350 – 1000cc handicap and he would not have liked, as limit man, having to be the first away. After a 'wobbly start', he still managed to lead for the first two laps, then was passed on the final lap by Munday's 495cc New Hudson, then by Knight on his big 976cc Zenith-JAP who swept past both men to win at 85.54mph. This still left a now more confident Wheeler having at least secured his first race placing.

At the Essex Motor Club's meeting on 9 May, Wheeler was to have a very satisfactory day, entering two of the three motorcycle races put on during this car race meeting. In the first three lap handicap for up to 500cc machines, Wheeler was able to take another third place. But it was in the 1000cc handicap race that he secured his first win on the Douglas, at a very creditable speed, for an amateur, of 80.72mph.

Wheeler was to ride consistently well in races throughout the 1925 season, finally recording a fastest lap of 86.62mph.

J S WRIGHT   980cc Zenith-JAP   18 July 1925

As we have seen on page 138, Wright began his racing career at Brooklands in 1924, winning his first race on a 249cc side-valve Zenith-JAP at a Public Schools MCC meeting in September that year. For the following year he had graduated to a 344cc Zenith-JAP, racing it in both solo form and with sidecar attached.

In 1925, here at the BMCRC's fourth meeting of the year, he appeared for the first time on a big Zenith, this one powered by the new short-stroke V-twin JAP racing engine, and caused an immediate sensation by raising the outer-circuit lap record for a motorcycle to 110.43mph.

By now most of the big Zenith machines were fitted, as here, with the Harley-Davidson front forks. Standing behind the front wheel, hand on hip, is the Zenith designer, Freddie Barnes, and on his right, in the white sweater, the private Zenith owner, H J Knight.

At the BMCRC meeting the following October, Wright, having won the 1000cc solo race at 102.90mph, raised eyebrows yet again by defeating Le Vack on his Brough Superior for the 1000cc sidecar championship, at 88.46mph.

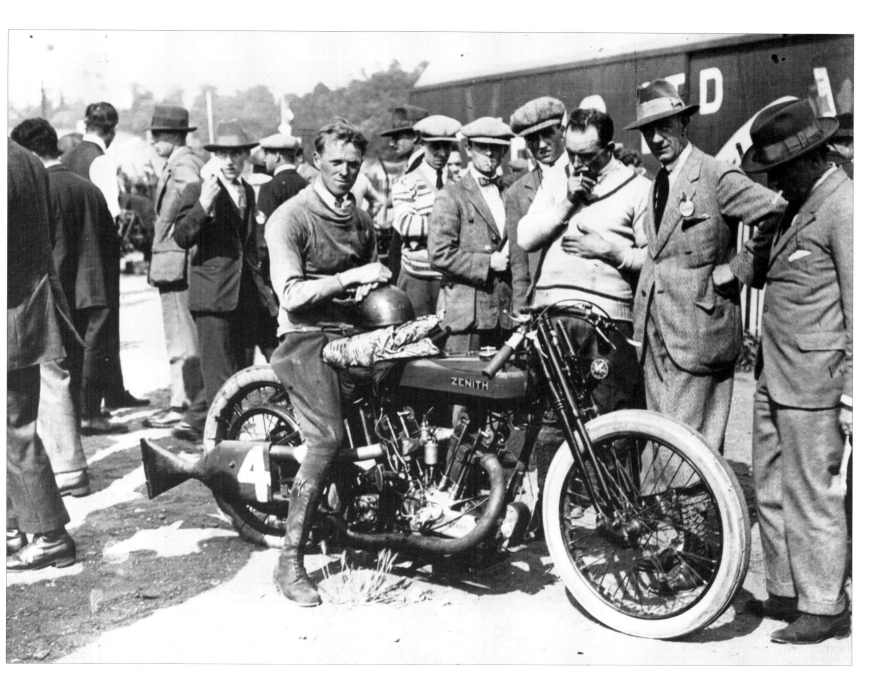

R KAYE DON   344cc Zenith-JAP   15 August 1925

Kaye Don had originally entered for the classic 200 mile races on 15 August 1925 intending to ride his 980cc Zenith in the 1000cc race in the afternoon. However, he had earlier injured an ankle and felt he would not really be up to coping with the big machine.

Freddie Barnes, the Zenith team manager, suggested he used the smaller, works 344cc machine in the 350cc race in the morning as an alternative and Don said he'd give it a try.

In the event, the race turned out to be a very lively affair, the lead changing hands frequently. Wal Handley took his Rex-Acme-Blackburne into the lead after thirty laps and, after a bewildering series of place changes, was to win at 78.37mph. Second place went to R H Hopkins on a 348cc Chater-Lea, Kaye Don managing to hang on to finish in third place.

An unpleasant incident in the race involved Dougal Marchant, the Chater-Lea specialist. Running steadily in second place, he hit one of the track's more notorious bumps and his unprotected chin hit the machine's front number plate. He was effectively knocked out, just managing to pull up before collapsing. A number of Brooklands riders around at the time were sporting one or more false teeth resulting from their face hitting the projecting parts on the tank, the forks or number plate of their machine as a result of the poor surface of the track.

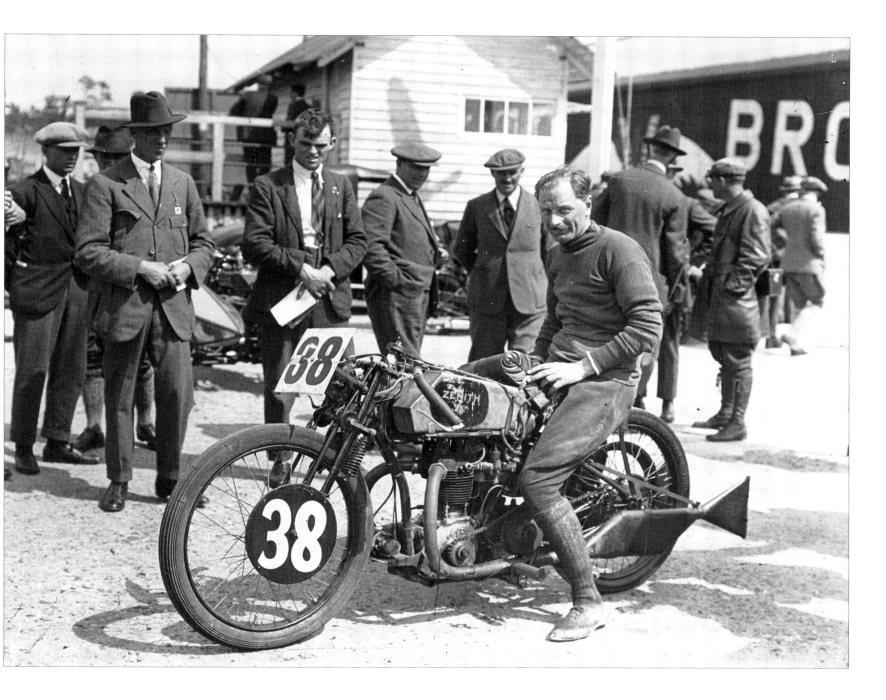

P G DALLISON   170cc Elfson-Norman   10 October 1925

Percy Dallison commenced his attack on long distance record in Class B, 175cc solo, in April 1924 when, riding a 170cc Omega-Norman, he established the flying start five miles and standing start 10 miles records at 57.32 and 50.37mph respectively.

For the following year, he had fitted one of the new overhead valve Norman engines to his Elfson machine and with it, in August, claimed a new 50 kilometres record at 62.3mph.

Encouraged by the speed of the new engine, he entered the 175cc solo championship race on 10 October 1925. From the start, he simply streaked away from Worters' record-breaking Cotton-Blackburne, to finish half a lap ahead. With a last lap at 72.07mph, he had succeeded in establishing four new records, the f/s five miles and five kilometres, and the s/s 10 miles and 10 kilometres. It is no wonder that, in the picture, he looks quietly pleased with himself.

The tiny engine in his Elfson, produced by the Norman Engineering Company of Leamington, had a bore and stroke of 60 x 60mm. Unlike the road-going model, this racing engine had a cast-iron, hemispherical combustion chamber cylinder head, held down through the rocker bridge, which was fitted with double-row roller bearings for each rocker.

The valves had a considerable angle of inclination, the inlet valve being larger than the exhaust. The pushrods were slightly inclined and had enclosed return springs, with the tappets being operated by separate cams and light internal rockers. The oil pump was driven from the inlet camshaft, whilst the exhaust camshaft carried a bevel gear for the magneto drive. The magneto lay at right angles to the crankshaft in front of the engine.

The crankshaft was unusual in being of the overhung type. A double-row roller bearing big end was fitted and the H-section connecting rod was attached to the piston by a fully floating gudgeon pin. The flywheel was outside, in the manner of Blackburne and Douglas engines.

G C COBBOLD   493cc Sunbeam   20 March 1926

Gordon Cobbold had started his Brooklands racing career with a long-stroke Sunbeam in the summer of 1924 but, after winning only his second race was not to attract much notice until the following year.

At a West Kent Motor Club meeting on 4 April 1925, Cobbold appeared on a 'semi-works' 493cc ohv Sunbeam tuned by Harry Weslake, on which he won two races. The first of these was for Sunbeam machines only and his winning speed was 82.31mph.

His next win was at the Sunbeam Club's own meeting on 13 June and this time he was riding a 593cc Sunbeam. This meeting was significant in that it was the last of the traditional small club events to be held at Brooklands. The local residents' case against the BARC for 'causing a nuisance' because of noise had been settled out of court, but only at the price of many minor club race meetings, mostly for motorcycles, being cancelled. Only the BARC, the BMCRC and one or two other major clubs were not affected.

Probably for this reason Cobbold does not appear in race reports until the opening BMCRC meeting of 1926, on 20 March. Many of the top riders were entered and, despite near freezing temperatures, a large crowd of spectators enjoyed exciting racing.

There were a number of uncomfortable moments for the competitors, too. Chater-Lea exponent Dougal Marchant badly gashing his chin over a bump, as already mentioned elsewhere in these pages, and another rider having his handlebars come away in his hands at over 90mph at the end of the Railway Straight, getting away with some bad bruising.

Here, Cobbold, reunited with the Weslake-tuned 493cc ohv Sunbeam, had won the three lap 350 -1000cc handicap race at 86.62mph. The fitting of a two-port engine into a sprint frame at that time was considered an unusual feature.

The bystanders in the picture taken after his win are clearly kitted out for the cold but sunny conditions on that March day.

G L WALLIS   344cc Wallis-JAP   10 April 1926

At the second BMCRC meeting of 1926, the talk of the paddock was a most unusual machine, the brainchild of George Wallis. It was powered by a 344cc JAP engine and was entered in the three lap 350cc solo handicap race.

Besides being the most unusual machine at the meeting, it was generally agreed to appear to be the best steering one. Onlookers and even other competitors in the race said it hardly ever appeared to waver from its course, even over the worst of the Brooklands bumps and Wallis gained a well-deserved second place behind Worters' 344cc Excelsior-JAP.

In the vintage years, many of the problems of fork rake and trail, indeed one of steering as a whole, remained to be solved. The patented Wallis design was a complete breakaway from the generally accepted motorcycle frame and steering principles.

The machine's front wheel was mounted inside a rigid triangular sub-frame on a special bearing, and was controlled by two vertical duplex tie-rods from the hub shell extremities to the steering-crown. Finally, two further horizontal tie-rods connected the steering-crown to the handlebar steering-arms.

A F HAMILTON   348cc Velocette   10 April 1926

Whilst undoubtedly the most unusual machine at the BMCRC's second meeting of 1926 was George Wallis' 344cc Wallis-JAP, another more normal development paid dividends in the first racing success for the one Velocette entered. Alec Hamilton's 348cc machine was the winner of the three lap private owners' handicap race at the excellent speed of 75.23mph.

With the introduction of their 348cc bevel driven, ohc single cylinder racing machine in 1924, it was clear that Veloce Ltd had fully appreciated, as had JAP's brilliant engine designer Val Page, as well as Marchant, that the limiting factors to four-stroke engine performance were the rate of operation of the valve gear and the heat of the exhaust valve or valves. In addition, a narrow crankcase and short, rigid crankshaft were necessary for reliability at the sustained high rpm and power output of which the engine would be capable.

Results were to prove the high quality of this brilliant, yet simple design, well into the future.

V E HORSMAN   599cc Triumph sidecar   26 June 1926

Spectators who turned out for the 200 mile sidecar races on Saturday 26 June 1926 would not have been impressed by the reliability of the day's track-racing motorcycle. Only five out of the field of seventeen competitors in the 350cc event finished the race. In the 600cc race, only one finished and, in the 1000cc category, none at all. Tyres, pistons, valves, carburettors, gearboxes – virtually every conceivable part gave someone trouble. Even the silencers which fell off or blew open would have led to retirement, given the stringent silencing regulations now being strictly enforced.

Seen on the far right, having been the sole finisher and thus the winner in the 600cc race, Victor Horsman would probably have won anyway, running as he was at record speeds throughout the race. His average speed for the 200 miles was 74.92mph.

Horsman's machine was the first Triumph he raced, having changed from Nortons in 1923. Even with sidecar attached, it still incorporated his winning formula of a long, low machine, running on alcohol fuel and tuned so as to be able to pull a higher top gear ratio than his rivals. In the inset picture below, Horsman had just won a three-lap 1000cc solo scratch race in May 1925, at a remarkable speed of 94.68mph.

C W G LACEY   344cc Grindlay Peerless-JAP   24 July 1926

The BMCRC staged its classic 200 mile solo races at the club's fifth meeting of 1926, in July. There were to be two outstanding performances during the meeting, both of them during the same race, that for 350cc solos.

C W G Lacey took his Grindlay Peerless into the lead before half way and held it, maintaining his usual steady lapping, always with a little in hand. The main drama was behind him.

Wal Handley, on his 348cc Rex-Acme-Blackburne, was about to go to the start when someone pointed out a long gash in the sidewall of his front tyre. Furious, for the gash could not possibly have occurred by accident, Handley set to and changed the cover. When he finally got under way on the track, he was no less than seven laps in arrears.

Clearly determined, he was going like a demon and, to everyone's surprise, was closing not only on the field but also on the leader, Bill Lacey. However, Lacey had too much in hand, keeping Handley at bay, and running out a delighted winner at 81.20mph.

Finishing in second place at an average speed only one mile an hour less than Lacey, Handley was found by the timekeepers to have broken ten distance and speed records, including a new 100 mile 350cc record, all at over 91mph.

Nothing, however, could diminish the winner's drama-free performance and here we see Lacey with his usual admiring throng, one of the hands on his shoulder belonging to his ever-supportive father, complete with waistcoat. The slightly sinister looking gentleman in the dark overcoat is clearly involved, although we do not know how. On the right in riding breeches, is the tall figure of Zenith-JAP sidecar specialist, Ted Baragwanath, one of Lacey's keenest supporters.

Perhaps it was on 'Barry's' recommendation that, for this race, Lacey had braced the loop frame of his machine with stays running from under the steering head to the engine plates.

J S WRIGHT   996cc Brough Superior-JAP   26 March 1927

The opening BMCRC meeting of 1927 saw difficult conditions due to heavy rain and gale-force winds. The 1000cc solo scratch race was put back to the afternoon as the track was now becoming treacherous. Despite these poor conditions, when the race did finally start, the private owner Joe Wright on his big Brough Superior romped away from the field, to win at 96.33mph, including one scorching lap at 102.90mph.

   As can be seen from the picture, Wright now preferred the standard Harley-Davidson front forks with a single Hartford shock absorber to those with Castle modifications as on the production SS100 Brough Superiors.

   Later that year, in September, Wright and Freddie Dixon took their Broughs to Arpajon in France to attack Temple's 1926 flying start kilometre record of 121.41mph on his OEC-Temple-Anzani. Their attempts failed, Wright recording 118.73mph and Dixon 118.98mph, with Dixon making the fastest one-way run of 119.11mph. The oft-repeated claim that Dixon averaged a fraction over 120mph, including a one-way run of 130mph, is not corfirmed by the official figures.

H G GROSE   347cc Matchless   10 April 1927

Gus Grose was to turn out to be a fine rider, once he had got over the painful results of the occasional tumble which most Brooklands riders would experience from time to time.

He is seen here on his first machine, a 347cc Matchless, on which he learned the ropes during 1927. His first success was to be in April 1928, riding his father's 346cc Excelsior-JAP, winning a three-lap 350cc solo handicap at 83.99mph. He followed that with another fine win in a handicap race, this one up to 1000cc, again on the family Excelsior, this time at a speed of 87.84mph.

His first outing on a sidecar outfit, a 588cc Norton, was in the gruelling 200 mile sidecar races in 1929, coming third in the 600cc race at 62.65mph. Later that year, now riding a Harry Weslake-tuned 493cc Sunbeam, he notched up two wins, one at 94.33mph.

He continued to ride a Weslake entry in 1930, this time a 499cc Rudge Whitworth, on which he lapped at over 100mph, so being rewarded with the coveted Brooklands Gold Star.

C W G LACEY 488cc Grindlay Peerless-JAP 20 April 1927

Somehow Bill Lacey had managed to 'fool' the handicappers for the three lap 350 -1000cc solo handicap here at the second BMCRC meeting of 1927, thus earning himself a more generous start in the following three-lapper , the '90mph race,' for riders who had achieved a lap at that speed.

This he won at 97.08mph, covering his second lap at 100.41mph. Thus he shared the 100mph lap honours with the two Berts, Denly and Le Vack, who were also competing.

Seen here after the race, Lacey's machine appears in its sprint race guise, with Webb forks and small capacity petrol tank.

Without doubt, it was Lacey who first combined showroom finish with mechanical perfection in the racing motorcycle, and this dull nickel-plated Grindlay could well have come from its stand at the Motor Cycle Show.

Wherever he went, Bill Lacey's machines earned unstinted praise, and at the Arpajon meeting of 1928 at the French track, his 498cc record breaker was considered to be the finest motorcycle yet seen in France: see page 202.

Somewhat 'defaced' by the top edge of the picture is Bill Lacey's father, in the pale jacket, as always posing proudly with his son.

A DENLY   490cc Norton   20 April 1927

In January 1927 RMN Spring took over the Norton activities at Brooklands as team manager with Bert Denly as rider. As soon as April the first records of the year were taken by the team, Denly breaking Class F (600cc s/car) records with this 490cc Norton up to 10 miles. Then, in solo trim, he achieved the highest speeds ever with a single cylinder motorcycle, the five miles at 105.77, and the five kilometres at 105.91mph, both from a flying start.

Later in the month, at the second BMCRC race meeting of 1927, Denly won the five lap 500cc solo race, just beating Bert Le Vack on his New Hudson. His average speed of 100.82mph made him the first rider of a Class C machine to win a race at over a hundred miles an hour. His speed for his second lap was 104.19mph.

Here is Denly on the Norton, celebrating his success with a quiet cigarette. The machine was Spring's brainchild, with its modified frame, Webb forks, 20 inch rim rear wheel and 22 inch front. The 490cc engine had a Chater-Lea connecting rod with 8.5 inches between centres instead of the standard 7 inches. This had required the use of a sleeved 588cc cylinder barrel with its three extra cooling fins, a special Martlet piston giving a compression ratio of about 9.5 to 1, and long-dwell cams.

An out and out special, the machine was miles an hour faster than the factory TT racers and was quite the most interesting Norton ever to be raced at Brooklands.

J S WORTERS   246cc Excelsior-JAP   20 April 1927

At the same BMCRC meeting on 20 April as Denly became the first 500cc rider to win a race at 100mph, J S Worters, usually known as 'Woolly', rode this Excelsior to win the three lap 1000cc solo experts' handicap at 84.84mph. He also won the three lap 350cc solo handicap at 86.62mph, remarkable speeds for a '250'.

Worters was another of the great engineer-riders to appear on the Brooklands scene, particularly in the vintage period. At the start of his career in 1924 he raced a '350', a Torunda-Blackburne, then a 248cc Cotton-Blackburne in 1925. On both he enjoyed considerable success, finally turning to preparing and racing Excelsiors with 246 and 346cc JAP engines.

1927 was the year that he was joined by C S Staniland, who rode for him, usually on Excelsiors, up until the end of the decade.

C S STANILAND   344cc Excelsior-JAP   9 July 1927

Chris Staniland started racing at Brooklands in 1923 on a two-stroke Velocette, scoring his first win on his first appearance at the track. The following year he was winning on one of his own Nortons, as a result of which he was soon competing on works Nortons, firstly those under O'Donovan, then with Spring.

In 1925 he won the 200 mile 600cc sidecar race on a 588cc Norton at 68.88mph and, in the following year, the BMCRC 750cc championship solo race, again on a 588cc Norton, at the rousing speed of 98.82mph.

In 1927 Staniland joined J S Worters, to compete on his team's Excelsior-JAP machines. He is seen here on his first appearance on a Worters entry, having won the 200 miles 350cc solo race at 83.42mph in pouring rain. His win was one of many in what would prove to be a highly successful partnership.

Earlier that afternoon Staniland had taken the lead in the 200 mile 500cc race on one of Spring's 490cc Nortons after Rex Judd had retired with a broken valve collar. Almost immediately, however, the very same trouble was to put Staniland out of the race, leaving the eventual win to a very surprised R Gibson on a 493cc Sunbeam.

The tall man in the raincoat standing on the right of the picture is probably Billy Wells, the one-time Indian racing team manager.

P BREWSTER   996cc Zenith-JAP sidecar   23 July 1927

For the BMCRC Cup Day on 23 July 1927, a most interesting 50 mile handicap sidecar race had been arranged for outfits up to 1000cc.

From the start it was clear that the veteran rider Phillip Brewster, better known as 'Percy', on his big Zenith machine had much more speed in hand than the handicappers had allowed for. Despite all the efforts of the scratch man, Bert Le Vack (592cc New Hudson sidecar), who tore round the track but could not catch him, Brewster came through the rest of the field to win at a dashing 88.47mph. Le Vack could only finish in fifth place.

In the picture, left to right, is Brewster, with Zenith designer Freddie Barnes, enjoying a victory cigarette; then the second place man, W Edwards on his 344cc Rex-Acme-JAP (64); and, finally, E S Prestwick, who took third place on a 344cc Coventry Eagle-JAP (55).

For several years Brewster had been selling racing pistons of his own design under the name Martlet. These aluminium alloy pistons were some of the earliest to incorporate such modern features as ribbed supports for the gudgeon-pin bosses and which had achieved great popularity with both car and motorcycle tuners.

Brewster was said to have designed a Martlet 998cc big-twin racing engine with a bore and stroke of 76x110mm. Both cylinder heads and barrels had finning parallel to the ground and were interchangeable between cylinders. This was the theme of the whole engine so as to be amenable to low-cost production, even though a racing unit.

Brewster entered a Zenith with the new engine installed at the first BMCMC meeting of 1925, but failed to make an appearance. Little is known of its subsequent history.

R N JUDD   494cc Douglas   27 August 1927

The decade from 1920 to the end of 1929 that is often referred to as the vintage years saw a number of top Brooklands tuner/riders move from one manufacturer's team to another; in some cases more than once.

Rex Judd, having enjoyed several successful years riding for the Norton concern under the guidance of D R O'Donovan, had moved in 1923 to the Douglas team as tuner and rider.

In April that year he made a most auspicious debut at the first BMCRC meeting, winning both the 350cc and 500cc races. By 1925, the new overhead valve 494cc Douglas now had its gearbox attached to the frame beneath the saddle. A box had been installed from which the two carburettors drew air, serving, in effect, as a crude pressure equalisation device.

By 1927 Judd had the Douglas thoroughly developed and, at the Hutchinson Hundred meeting on 27 August, he is seen here having won the three lap winners' handicap race at 98.62mph and the five lap 90mph handicap race at 99.61mph, his last lap being completed at 103.54mph. In fact Judd was to remain as the only rider of a 500cc Douglas to have lapped Brooklands at over 100mph in the vintage years.

Judd's fine performances at this meeting were disappointingly clouded by his withdrawal from the main race of the day in protest against the handicapper's decision to base the handicap of his entry, on another Douglas, on his speeds on the machine he had ridden in the earlier races.

F W DIXON 996cc Brough Superior-JAP 27 August 1927

Here we see Dixon on the one-off 996cc Brough Superior entered for the Hutchinson Hundred race on 27 August 1927. Unfortunately, he was put out early in the race with tyre trouble.

Resplendent in nickel plate, this machine had a redesigned frame incorporating a very massive steering head, extra bracing stays running between the chain stays and cradle tubes, and a cross-member at the base of the front down tube receiving the cradle tubes in two separate lugs at each of its extremities, as in F W Barnes' Zenith frames. The front forks were webbed for extra strength, and had two independent handlebars attached, one to each fork blade, as on Dixon's eight-valve Harley-Davidson.

At the Arpajon Speed Trials in September 1927, Dixon attained a speed of 130mph on three occasions; but owing to failure of the timing strips, these speeds were not ratified by the organisers. George Brough was equally unfortunate with the machine the following year, when he recorded 130.60mph in one direction over the flying kilometre, only to be put out by mechanical trouble on the return run. However, on 1 September 1929, in the hands of Le Vack, the same machine raised the coveted record to 129.06mph.

At the BMCRC championship meeting in September 1927, Dixon won the 1000cc sidecar race on the Brough at 91.72mph, and later the three lap all-comers passenger handicap race at 95.78mph, during which he lapped at over 100mph, the first occasion a passenger machine had achieved this feat at Brooklands.

H Le VACK   496cc New Hudson   23 June 1928

The year 1926 opened on a very sad note for those connected with Brooklands with the death in January of the track's builder and owner, H J Locke King. This came at a time when a downturn in the country's economic climate was already effecting industry in general. The motorcycle manufacturers were also feeling the pinch, the closure of the J A Prestwich racing department being just one early sign of the times.

Bert Le Vack, who had been with JAPs since 1922, now moved to the New Hudson Motor Cycle Company to take over racing design. In due course he had produced four new machines specifically for outer circuit racing. These would be of 346, 496, and 655cc capacity for solo use, and one of 591cc for sidecar events.

Le Vack always raced his own creations. By early 1927, development work on the new 496cc machine had reached such a stage that, on 20 April he was able to take second place behind Denly's Norton in a five-lap 500cc solo scratch race. By averaging 100.82mph, Denly became the first rider of a 500cc machine to win a race at over 100mph, with one lap at 104.19mph. Immediately after the race, Le Vack, not to outdone, wheeled out another New Hudson, on which he beat Denly's record, at 105mph.

Le Vack only once raced the largest, 655cc New Hudson, which had the 82mm bore of its smaller brother, with a stroke of 124mm. The event was a three lap experts' solo handicap race, on 14 April 1928, which Le Vack won, according to him, "on the pilot jet", at 103.97mph, with one lap at 108.88mph. Presumably the main jet was used for that particular lap.

In the picture we see him having won his last race at the track, the 200 mile 500cc solo race, during the BMCRC's fifth meeting of 1928. His winning speed was 94.85mph, which also gave New Hudson two new Class C records, the two hours, and 200 miles.

Shortly after this record-breaking win, New Hudson Limited discontinued its Brooklands racing programme and, to all intents and purposes, Le Vack's long career at Brooklands ended here.

C W G LACEY 499cc Grindlay Peerless-JAP 1 August 1928

We have already come across Bill Lacey in these pages a number of times, primarily because of his long and successful career dating from his first win in 1924, riding his neat 344cc Cotton-JAP. The description of neat does not really do him justice, for his machines were not only very fast, but superbly prepared and turned out.

Having in 1925 talked Reg Grindlay into providing him with a machine to replace his little Cotton, Lacey was to do Grindlay Peerless proud over the next five years, consistently winning races on both the 350 and 500cc versions of his Grindlay, and breaking many records, including, at Arpajon in France, the flying start kilometre for both capacity classes, at 104.12 and 112.16mph.

Finally, at Brooklands on 1 August 1928, he won the 'Motor Cycle' silver cup for the first rider to cover 100 miles in one hour on British soil, by putting 103 miles and 532 yards behind him in the sixty minutes on the magnificent motorcycle pictured, with Lacey, on the opposite page.

In 1971, the author of this book came across the remains of an old racing motorcycle. Joseph Bayley believed it to be the long lost Bill Lacey machine, and Lacey himself confirmed that it was. The fully restored Grindlay Peerless finally returned to the track at the Brooklands Reunion of 1984, where it was to be ridden again on the Byfleet Banking. Below, the machine is being critically inspected at the event by 'Titch' Allen and a still sprightly Bert Denly.

E C E BARAGWANATH   996cc Brough Superior-JAP   8 September 1928

Baragwanath raced Zenith, P & P and Brough Superior sidecar outfits at Brooklands during the 1920s as well as competing in the many speed trials and hill climbs which were so popular in the vintage period in particular.

But it was on his big Brough Superior-JAP outfits that he was to become famous. On his first machine, one of the fabulous SS100s, he made an unsuccessful debut at the BMCRC Easter meeting in 1925, but scored his first win a month later. He won the 1000cc sidecar championship at 85.48mph in September 1926 and repeated this success in 1928. Between these two was his 200 mile 1000cc sidecar race

victory in 1927 at 73.95mph. Baragwanath is seen here in the picture having won the five lap 1000cc sidecar event at the September 1928 BMCRC championship meeting at a speed of 84.56mph.   His sidecar passenger could well be Bert Le Vack, but as few if any of the sidecar occupants got a mention in race reports it is difficult to be sure.

Usually known as Barry, Baragwanath was a brilliant tuner who was always ready to help or advise other competitors. One of Brooklands' greatest characters, he could be easily be recognised by the stiff, three inch high wing collar he always wore, even when racing.

C J WILLIAMS 495cc Raleigh 23 March 1929

After his successful association with Nortons, O'Donovan joined Raleighs, primarily to design their TT machines. However, his Brooklands experience led to the appearance of this formidable track motorcycle on 21 April 1928. The rider, Jack Williams, was quite unable to demonstrate its potential due to pouring rain which led to the meeting being abandoned.

However, in the 200 mile race on 23 June that year, a splendid battle developed between Williams on the new Raleigh and Le Vack on his New Hudson, both lapping at over 100mph. Unhappily, the Raleigh's silencer was to come adrift, the new strict silencing regulations giving Williams no choice but to retire an otherwise fully raceworthy machine.

Here we see Williams on 23 March 1929 having won a three lap 500cc scratch race at 98.43mph, a few lengths ahead of Paddy Johnston's Cotton-Blackburne. Both riders covered their second laps at the identical speed of 102.33mph.

Williams also gave the 598cc Raleigh its first outing at the track, coming fourth in the experts' handicap race. For the second lap, he averaged 108.98mph, which not only spoiled Le Vack's day by equalling his Class D record on the 655cc New Hudson, but also demonstrated the new machine's potential.

In 1930, in the Hutchinson Hundred race on 30 October, Williams brought the 495cc Raleigh home, only in fourth place, but still at 103.22mph, the fastest average speed of any machine in the history of that classic handicap race.

After the 1939-45 war, Jack Williams was to become the AJS and Matchless chief racing development engineer. In due course his son Peter was also to make his mark, both as a rider and a design engineer.

Such is the heritage of Brooklands.

J S WRIGHT   996cc Zenith-JAP 23 March 1929

At the BMCRC opening meeting of 1929, on 23 March, for the three lap 350-1000cc solo handicap, Bert Denly came to the line on a machine powered by the largest single-cylinder engine ever seen at the track, an ohc 743cc AJS with the incredible dimensions of 84x134mm.

Unhappily for Denly, however, Joe Wright was also present with his big Zenith, and in top form, having covered the flying start kilometre in practice that morning at over 120mph. Starting from scratch, Wright won the race, completing his three laps at 95.78, 113.71 and 113.19mph, the second being a new Brooklands motorcycle lap record.

In the picture, Wright is seen after the race with Claude Temple, in the tweed jacket, his one time race adversary and now business partner. This machine had been presented to them both by the debenture holders of Zenith Motors before the company went into liquidation, in appreciation of their services to motorcycling.

The frame is probably from the works Zenith originally raced by Wright in 1926, now with Temple's modifications, including bracing stays on both sides of the front down tube and the replacement of the Harley-Davidson leading link front forks by Druid girders.

Though by no means a dour man, this is probably the only photograph of Wright where he is caught smiling, albeit not broadly.

G H TUCKER   588cc Norton sidecar   4 May 1929

Here is the ever-smiling George Tucker on his Norton having just won the 1000cc sidecar race in the BMCRC championship meeting in May 1929 at an average speed of 84.13 mph. Earlier he had come second behind Bert Denly's 598cc ohc AJS outfit in the 600cc sidecar race. To finish off a perfect day, Tucker would win the final event, the five lap all-comers passenger handicap for the 'Wakefield Cup', at 84.84 mph.

Perhaps the most remarkable aspect of his story is that one has to go back almost eight years, to August 1921, to find his first win, even then driving a Norton sidecar outfit, but of course a flat tank, side-valve 490cc machine.

Although also a fine rider of solos, it was in long-distance sidecar racing that Tucker excelled, as seen by his record in the series of classic 200 mile events. Always in the 600cc class, he won the race on 17 June 1922, a feat he repeated in 1924 and 1929. In addition to these three victories, he was placed second on four other occasions.

In road racing, too, he had made his mark, winning the 600cc and 1000cc classes in the 1923 Belgian Sidecar Grand Prix, and the Isle of Man Sidecar TT in 1924.

J S Wright 996cc Zenith-JAP 20 April and 1 June 1929

At the second BMCRC race meeting of 1929, on Saturday 20 April, a series of races featured winners coming home as far as half a mile ahead of the second place rider.

Most of these races were, frankly, rather boring. But one, the three lap 350-1000cc solo handicap race, was definitely not. The winner, Joe Wright on his big Zenith, put on a thrilling performance from scratch, hugging the outside perimeter all the way round the Members' and Byfleet Bankings, to win easily at 111.52mph.

This was the highest motorcycle race speed yet at Brooklands. After a standing start lap at 103.76mph, Wright is seen here, on his second lap, about to set yet another new motorcycle lap record of 117.19mph . On his final lap, with nobody to chase, he eased off the throttle.

Two weeks later, at the fourth BMCRC race meeting, Wright entered the same solo handicap race as last time. Having again had to start from scratch on his Zenith, he is pictured, on the far right, going flat out, well inside the ten-foot line on the reverse bend through the Fork, in hot pursuit of the two 493cc Sunbeams ridden by Gus Grose, with 51 seconds start, and Kirby, with 54 seconds.

With a standing lap at 102.06mph, Wright yet again broke the outright motorcycle record with his second at 118.86mph, but losing to Grose at the finish by two machine lengths. His new record lap would not be broken until 1935. His race speed, 112.33mph, will remain unbeaten.

A DENLY   346cc AJS   27 July 1929

Over the winter Nigel Spring had moved his team from Norton to the AJS concern and the new chromium plated models were all given their first outing at the opening meeting of 1929. Bert Denly had stayed with the Spring equipe and was entered at the meeting on all four machines, 346cc, 494cc and 743cc solos, plus a 598cc sidecar outfit. Although much admired by other riders and spectators alike, none of the machines lived up to the standard of their appearance at their first outing.

On 27 July, however, the chain-driven overhead camshaft 346cc AJS gave Spring the first sniff of success when, at the BMCRC 200 mile solo races, Denly won the 350cc race at 89.20mph. They are seen here after the race with a number of onlookers no doubt admiring the handsome lines of the machine. The following September, at Arpajon in France, on the same model, Denly raised the flying-start kilometre record to 107.02mph.

In 1930 Spring's team was strengthened by the addition of Hicks and Baker, Hicks winning that year's 350cc 200 mile sidecar race at 73.12mph, and Baker the 350cc 200 mile solo race at 91.58mph.

The culminating triumph, however, was to be Denly's, when the following October, this time at Monthlery, he covered 104.25 miles in one hour on the self same 346cc AJS. Some time later, whilst running-in one of Spring's new AJS machines, Denly found himself circulating virtually side by side with Captain George Eyston doing the same thing with the latest 2.3 litre Grand Prix Bugatti.

Comparing notes in the pits afterwards, Eyston asked Denly if he would be interested in completing the running-in of the Bugatti. This in turn led to Denly becoming Eyston's chief engineer, being responsible for preparing his many record breaking cars, and managing the successful attempt at Bonneville in 1938 on the World Land Speed Record with his huge 'Thunderbolt' car, at 357.5mph.

G E NOTT   499cc Rudge Whitworth   27 July 1929

Ernie Nott appeared on the Brooklands scene like a meteor, and immediately proceeded to travel like one on his works tuned four-valve 499cc Rudge Whitworth.

On 19 October 1928, he won the Buckley Cup, put up for the first rider to cover 200 miles inside two hours, by achieving the distance with some seventeen seconds to spare. Earlier that month, in a five lap 500cc solo race, he had won his Brooklands 'Gold Star' with a lap at 100.27mph.

In November 1929 he was to raise the classic hour record to 106 miles and 432 yards and, in the same month, in partnership with team colleague Tyrrell Smith, covered 205 miles and 1584 yards in two hours.

Between these bouts of high-speed record breaking he ran away with the 1929 200 mile 500cc solo race at 100.07mph and he is seen in the picture with his purposeful looking machine in the Paddock before the start.

It was customary in those days to take the winner's picture after the race; quite evidently the photographer had no illusions about the result of this one.

C S STANILAND   248cc Rex-Acme-Blackburne   5 April 1930

Throughout 1930, J S Worters, Chris Staniland's entrant, used the new Blackburne engines of 248cc, 348cc and 498cc capacity, in Cotton, Excelsior, Rex-Acme and Zenith frames. The engines became best known for the closely positioned parallel pushrods.

Here we see Staniland having won the one lap sprint scratch race on his 248cc machine at the BMCRC's twenty-first anniversary meeting in April 1930, at a speed of 78.43mph. At the same meeting, on Worters' 348cc Zenith- Blackburne, Staniland won the three lap solo handicap race for Classes A and B at 95.59mph, and 'The Motor Cycle' invitation race over three laps at 96.90mph. The machine's forks have been 'faired-in' with the use of tape, in the interests of streamlining.

Years later, Worters was to recall his career at Brooklands in a recording made for his old friend Charles Mortimer. Of Staniland he said: "Chris's idea of motorcycle or car racing was to turn up a few minutes before the first race, beautifully attired in spotless overalls and helmet. He had a mechanic push the bike out to the line and say to me 'Will this one win, Woolly?' and then ride as perfectly a race as humanly possible, with the throttle hard against the stop, come in, make some pertinent remarks on the bike, then go off to talk to other riders or friends, repeating the performance as necessary throughout the afternoon. A marvellous rider and friend. His car driving and flying were all of the same type and the Lord knows why he had to get killed in an unexplained accident."

Staniland had also been racing a Bugatti car at the track since 1926 and was to drive the Multi-Union single seater racing car built for him by Worters in 1938 in which he took the Class D, (3 litre) Brooklands lap record at 141.45mph.

A test-pilot in the RAF, Staniland was killed in 1942 in the unexplained flying accident to which Worters referred.

O M BALDWIN 980cc Zenith-JAP 27 June 1931

This was the third BMCRC members' meeting of 1931, originally planned for the 16 May, but postponed because of torrential rain.

One of the features of many of the club's race meetings were three lap motorcycle versus car challenge races and, on this occasion and at short notice, H W Purdy's old Thomas Special racing car was paired with Oliver Baldwin's 980cc Zenith-JAP.

The car had been built by the late Parry Thomas in 1926 and had become known as the 'Flat Iron' because of its low build. Baldwin had been competing at Brooklands since 1913, his first race that year on a 986cc BAT-JAP bringing him a third place in a 1000cc scratch race. Ever since he was to ride only big V-twins, for a time a MAG-engined Matchless, then becoming faithful to Zenith-JAP machines.

His first real success was sharing a new track lap record of 113.45 mph with Joe Wright's similar machine at the BMCRC's fixture in April 1926. For the following year, Baldwin had a new Zenith with the 996cc JAP engine which appeared to steer and handle better than any other big twin on the outer circuit. In 1928, at the annual speed trials at Arpajon in France, Baldwin set up a new world's record for the flying-start kilometre with a speed of 124.62mph. The metric equivalent, 200.67kph, was greeted with great enthusiasm there as 200kph had always represented to the French an impossible speed for a motorcycle.

Now up against the Thomas Special, however, Baldwin's straight line record speed was no match for Purdy who had got the old car going really well, lapping in recent car races at over 120mph, and now about to enjoy an easy win.

Here, on the first lap, Baldwin, followed by the low-slung car, has just hit the notorious bump on leaving the Members' Banking. At this sort of speed, his big machine will become fully airborne for up to fifty yards.

C B BICKELL   497cc Bickell-JAP   15 August 1931

At the BMCRC's fifth members' meeting of 1931, Ben Bickell, on his by now well-known Bickell-JAP, ran out the winner in the nine lap handicap race for the Capt Phillips Cup. His speed was 102.48mph. He had already earned his Gold Star by lapping the track at over 100mph at an earlier BMCRC meeting, and,during the forthcoming season of 1932, Bickell would go on to lap the outer circuit at over 112mph on his fine machine.

The brothers Bickell, Ben and Joe, ran a motorcycle business in Archway Road, Highgate in North London. One of the classic stories told about them at the time concerned an AA patrolman's Chater-Lea sidecar outfit which had become somewhat bent and was deposited at the Archway Road workshop for attention.

The sidecar, loaded with all sorts of equipment for rescuing motorists, was fit for service. The motorcycle was definitely not.

Joe Bickell decided that he could make a good job of the bent Chater-Lea which seemed to him to offer some racing potential. After due attention to the frame and the addition of bracing torque tubes, he had the frame, forks, tank and wheels copper-plated. Having fitted a potent 498cc JAP dirt-track engine to complete his side of the transformation, he handed the riding of the machine over to his brother, Ben.

Carrying on the Lacey tradition of mechanical excellence combined with showroom finish, the Bickell-JAP, under its nickname 'Copperknob', was to become perhaps the best-known of the many Brooklands specials.

E C E BARAGWANATH 996cc Brough Superior-JAP 15 August 1931

We have met 'Barry' before, the tough yet companiable tuner/rider of big V-twin Brough sidecar outfits since the early twenties (see Page 204). Now, for his last couple of years in active competition at Brooklands, he had prepared the final version of his magnificent machine, now fitted with a supercharger.

Mounted in front of the engine, the chain-driven Powerplus instrument had a car type carburettor fitted underneath together with its own oil pump. The bulk of the blower can just be seen, protected by a steel case from concrete chips thrown from the front wheel.

Not so easy to see are the two additional 'star' dampers fitted to the sides of the Harley-Davidson front forks. Each has a connecting strut attached to the bottom link of the forks. The usual Hartford shock absorber above the front wheel has been retained.

On this formidable machine Baragwanath was to lap the outer circuit many times at over 100mph. In 1933, on 29 July, he won a three lap senior handicap race at 99.21mph, with one lap at 103.97mph, a new Class G record.

Shortly after, having celebrated his fiftieth birthday, Barry had decided not to race again at Brooklands. He ran the Brough just once more, at the Brighton Speed Trials that year.

The story of the Baragwanath Brough had not ended, however, as in the hands of its new owner Noel Pope, the machine was to appear many more times in the record books.

A L LOWETH   497cc Loweth-JAP   19 September 1931

During the BMCRC sixth members' meeting of 1931, the five lap 1000cc handicap race for the Wakefield Cup was won by A L Loweth at an average speed of 103.97mph.

Loweth was numbered among the top flight of Brooklands riders and is best remembered for the remarkable speeds he extracted from his 490cc side-valve Norton, initially at a meeting in 1925 put on by the Sutton Coldfield and North Birmingham Auto Club, the first event at the track to be organised by a Midlands club.

His last race of the vintage period was in September 1929, winning a three lap 350-500cc race at 94.15mph, now with an ohv engine fitted to his old Norton. One lap was recorded at a fraction of a second over 100mph, thus winning him the coveted Brooklands Gold Star.

Loweth's new mount resulted from his Norton engine blowing up earlier in 1931. The JAP engine seen here was apparently advertised as the New JAP Special Competition Motor.

Originally designed for dirt track racing, the engine quickly proved to be equally suitable for Brooklands use. Priced at £50, one got the engine complete with a special ML magneto with Lissen sparking plug and lead, Amac carburettor, exhaust pipe, engine shaft shock absorber, engine plates and exhaust lifter control.

Further evidence of this new JAP engine being equally at home on the track as on dirt was to come the following year when W J C Hewitt, with a Worters-tuned New JAP engine fitted to his Excelsior, would raise the 500cc lap record to 115.29mph, as described on page 230.

The 100 Miles Junior Grand Prix Race   23 July 1932

Of the two 100 mile Grand Prix races on 23 July 1932, the first was for machines up to 350cc. The Senior event, at the end of the day, was for the up to 500cc category. The winner of the Junior race was H G Tyrell-Smith on a 349cc Rudge Whitworth, at an average speed of 70.64mph.

Les Archer was entered in both races on the supercharged 348cc Velocette owned by H J Willis. Here, in the first event, he has stopped for fuel whilst leading the race for 30 of the total 36 laps. Then plug trouble intervened, to drop him to third place at the finish.

Having rectified the plug problem in the break between races, Archer was to finish second in the final race, the Senior Grand Prix.

This supercharged machine made its first appearance in 1931, when the chain-driven Foxwell blower was outside the carburettor. The balancing chamber was in between, the whole fuel system of tank, carburettor and chamber being pressure balanced.

This arrangement proved to be clearly impractical and, in 1932, the carburettor was attached directly to the blower with the balancing chamber between that and the inlet port. It was in this more conventional form when the Velocette was raced by Archer at this meeting. It was neither raced nor seen again.

The 100 Miles Senior Grand Prix Race   23 July 1932

Two of the Douglas team riders are seen rounding the temporary chicane in the early laps of the Senior Grand Prix. On the left is C S Williams and, on the right, C W 'Paddy' Johnston. Veteran Frank Longman, who had first raced at Brooklands in 1920 on a 499cc Ariel, was the third member of the Douglas equipe and is not yet in view.

All of the Douglas engines had been modified by 'Woolly' Worters. But it was to be handling and brake troubles that slowed all three riders. A fourth Douglas, ridden by the amateur J H Fell, was to finish fourth. The winner was Ernie Knott on his 499cc Rudge Whitworth, at a speed of 72.54mph. As we saw on the previous page,

Les Archer on Willis' blown 348cc Velocette came home in second place.

During the interval between the two Grand Prix races, Williams won the three lap senior handicap race on a 494cc Douglas from the 30 second mark at 102.06mph. It was in this closely-fought race that W J C Hewitt and Ben Bickell lapped at 115.29 and 112.17mph respectively, in so doing both breaking Bert Denly's long-standing record of 111.42mph set up on Spring's 495cc AJS in October 1929.

Hewitt was riding a 498cc Excelsior-JAP, Bickell his 497cc Bickell-JAP. Remarkably, Hewitt's name has never appeared in the BMCRC list of 500cc Gold Star holders.

The Hutchinson Hundred Handicap Race   1 October 1932

The conditions for this 100 mile, thirty seven lap race were quite atrocious, heavy rain falling throughout the event. Such were the conditions that only seven of the twenty-nine starters finished within the time limit.

The winner was Ben Bickell, on his 497cc Bickell-JAP, seen here being congratulated after the race, his average speed being a remarkable 99.61mph.

Throughout the race, Bickell showed that his Brooklands 'special' was both fast and reliable and his control of the machine when, lap after lap, it would slide away from the Vickers sheds at the Fork, was an exhibition of the art of track racing in the wet of the highest order.

The picture on the far right shows him moving to overtake J A Baker, on a 346cc AJS (7), the second place rider, six laps from the end of the thirty-seven lap race. Despite the poor quality of the photograph, it is just possible to make out the spray streaming back from the top of Bickell's crash helmet.

M B SAUNDERS   246cc Excelsior-JAP   26 August 1933

Since setting up a Class A (250cc) record in October 1931 on his ex-Worters Excelsior, Saunders' ambition was to be the first to win a Gold Star for a lap at 100mph on a '250'.

Experiments with this partial streamlining at the front of the Excelsior, across the page, showed that even this made full throttle racing in anything other than good weather conditions difficult. With the complete Worters-designed shell installed, however, in anything other than totally calm conditions it could be disastrous.

Some eighteen months after setting his earlier record, the weather on 26 August 1933 was finally judged to be ideal. So, with full enclosure in place (inset), Saunders could now at last try to achieve his ambition. In a three lap all comers' handicap race he finished third behind Mortimer and Eves. His lap speeds were 88.15, 102.27 and 102.48mph, thereby winning the first and only Gold Star in Class A. Both his race and lap records would remain unbroken when Brooklands closed for ever in 1939.

In October 1932, L J Archer had in fact become the first rider of a '250' to exceed 100mph when, on a specially-prepared 246cc New Imperial, he set up Class A records over the flying start five kilometres and five miles at 100.38mph and 100.32mph. Unfortunately he did not win a Gold Star as these records were not set during a BMCRC race meeting.

S WOOD   492cc New Imperial   1 August 1934

The announcement of the 'The Motor Cycle' trophy for the first multi-cylinder 500cc machine to cover 100 miles in the hour had not only caught the attention of the Bickell brothers, as mentioned on page 248 , but also the racing department of the New Imperial concern.

They had already experimented with two of their 250cc racing engine cylinders on a common crankcase, which had shown both speed and reliability in the Isle of Man. But the machine in which the new engine had been fitted did not have the handling which the TT course demanded. Brooklands, however, was possibly another matter, so it was with some optimism that New Imperial Motors brought one of their IoM twin 500s to the track with 'Ginger' Wood being given the riding responsibilities.

In the initial sorting out period, the machine displayed some of the familiar handling vagaries, not helped by the short wheelbase which was unsuited to Brooklands. The roughness of the track was yet another matter.

Observers at the trials said it was terrifying to watch. Wood in particular was puzzled by an eerie 'yelp' he heard sometimes when holding the machine high up on the Home Banking on full song. Bystanders put the noise down to the wind, or reflection of sound from the inner wall or from the underside of the bridge.

In the end, reportedly as a result of pictures taken during the trials, Wood's 'yelp' turned out to be the front tyre reconnecting with the concrete when the steering was on partial lock, from a combination of inherent bad handling and the bumpy Brooklands surface.

On 1 August 1934, however, the weather conditions were perfect and the New Imperial was behaving impeccably. So much so that Wood was able to settle down right away to lapping at a steady 105mph, even that early being able to build up time in hand.

In his final stint after the scheduled fuel stop, he closed out the hour with laps between 100 and 102mph, his average speed for the sixty minutes being 102.22 mph, thus winning the 'The Motor Cycle' cup for New Imperial.

Hutchinson Hundred Day   25 August 1934

Competitors line up for the start of the three lap al- comers handicap race during a day of races offering good enough prize money to attract most of the regulars.

One who was yet to join that select band was newcomer Miss Beatrice Shilling, seen here on her Norton, three machines from the left. A report on how she fared is on page 242.

On her left on the start line is the just visible 996cc Brough Superior of Charles Mortimer, awaiting one of his first outings on the elderly machine he had recently bought from Geoffrey Davies. Fortunately for us, Mortimer was to recall his race in detail in one of his books.

Mortimer wrote as follows: "There were twenty-five starters, ranging in size from our 'thousand' down to a 175cc two-stroke. The distance was over three laps – eight and a quarter miles. We were not on the scratch mark – there was one behind us – Ben Bickell on his 350cc Bickell JAP and from Ben we were to receive just three seconds start in three laps. At that time Ben held the 350cc outer-circuit lap record on this bike at over 102 mph and we knew that if he was going to equal this we should have to lap at 101mph or more to beat him. At this time, the best lap we had done with the Brough in a race was well under 100mph. Among the twenty-three men to

whom we were giving a start, there were almost certainly dark horses. On the handicapping as it stood, the limit man on the 175 two-stroke would have to lap at around 65mph to win.

"No snags with the warming up. Sump drained, racing plugs fitted after warming up on soft ones – push up to the start line alongside the Vickers sheds. Some rudery from Ben about having to give start to a 'thousand' but, in fact, we knew that we should almost be departing together, so much heavier was the Brough for the two pushers to launch off the mark. Now we are ready and waiting for 'Ebby' to come along and brief us and he starts way down at the other end of the line opposite the timing box. Up the line he comes and we can hear his voice. 'You two together, you on your own, you four five-hundreds together.' Then he arrives. 'You on your own, Charles, and then you, Ben.'

"He returns to the other end of the line and after a moment's delay there is a flurry and the 175 bursts into life and starts its long journey towards the home banking facing us. A temptation to turn on the fuel is resisted, for the 'baby' will be droning along on his own for some time before anyone else leaves. We watch him toiling up the rise to the banking, the buzz of the tiny engine gradually fading. Now he is

out of sight and still we wait. Suddenly there is activity again as two 250's and a sidecar outfit depart together. Then two more solos and a roar as about five 350's depart in a tight bunch. Johnny's voice can just be heard above the din: 'Fuel on, Charlie.' In gear, now goggles down and waiting – he's almost here. The flag drops for the four 500's and Ebby jumps back nimbly, standing beside us. Watch his face – it's impassive, nothing to be gained there. Suddenly the flag is aloft and falls as quickly. For a moment nothing seems to happen except for a shuffling of feet. Now is the moment when the weight of a big twin becomes apparent, for we actually saw Ebby jump back to stand beside Ben. Our big engine is turning, but not fast enough to be able to drop the compression lever. Now it is, and as we drop it – there is an almighty bang from the exhaust and she fires. She takes a second to really take hold and in that split second we can actually hear Ben's engine to the right and almost alongside – dreadful!

"At last we are really moving – change into second – good, we're still on both cylinders, and now we really are going, climbing up on to the home banking as though we were in a lift. Should like to look astern to see if Ben's there but it's too risky, so concentrate on line

from now on. Into top at peak revs and already it's becoming hard work to keep the old lady on course. Bumps, bumps, bumps, bigger and better and causing the old bike to lurch and twist as she makes her way right up to the top line – within ten feet from the top of the banking. We sweep under the Members' Bridge and, having done so, can see nearly the whole way round the track. Not a bike in sight! No time to worry about that, we must get exactly positioned to negotiate the big bump over the bridge that spans the River Wey – to be wrongly placed there means trouble with a capital T. Here the bike becomes airborne for forty or fifty yards and must land dead straight at the beginning of the Railway straight. It does and now, for a moment, we can relax as we thunder down the straight at between 110 and 112mph. A quick scan round the horizons reveals nothing – the boys must all be miles away – it just can't be done. But, really, we know it can, for the bike is going as it's never gone before and these first two laps are our chance because there's bound to be a lot of traffic to get through on the third. Line it up, now, for the Byfleet banking and we go on far faster than ever before and, again, have that wonderful sensation of climbing in a lift. Round the Byfleet, high, high up, pulling it down slowly about three hundred yards from the end, so that the kink, at the fork, alongside the Vickers sheds will be ironed out and there'll be room for Ben to pass between us and the sheds, if he wants to. But there's no sign of him, which isn't surprising for had we known it, our standing lap had been turned at over 93mph, despite the hand gear change – outer circuit bikes hadn't aspired to foot change in those days!

"Across the wide expanse at the fork, a breathtaking lift up on to the tighter home banking, and one or two stragglers are being passed – earlier than we would have expected. Again the big bump, the Railway straight and the Byleet and now they can be seen. Bikes by the dozen it seems, way ahead on the banking, the leaders streaming off the banking and across the fork. Some are a long way ahead but we're coming up on them fast. Passed two or three across the fork but the home banking looks like the Brighton road on a Sunday. This is the difficult bit, for everyone is using the banking here and the faster 500's are using the top. They're nearly all lapping at over the ton and our second lap was done at nearly 106mph. The bike's too big to weave in and out of them but we have to pass beneath two who are using far more of the banking than they need for their lap speeds of around 103 or 104mph. Even so, they were so high that we barely had to pull the bike down at all and we were lucky in that they could be seen a long way ahead.

"Some of the limit people seem to be crawling as we thunder past them down the Railway Straight for the last time, and as we enter the Byfleet there is no longer anyone else to be seen. Now that we're on the Byfleet again and, emerging from the Hawker sheds, we can see all the way to the finishing line – still not a bike in sight. Automatically we ease – but only momentarily, opening up again instantly on the thought that Ben could well be right astern. Now across the line – chequered flag and we ease, surprised that, with the problems of passing on that last lap, we had completely forgot the problems of handling the bike.

"The race had been won at an average of 100.82mph from a standing start and had taken just five minutes from start to finish. Crawling by today's standards, but exciting nearly forty years ago on bumpy old Brooklands."

As a result of this race Charles Mortimer joined the select group of 1000cc Gold Star holders. It is interesting to compare Mortimer's experience with that of young P J Wallace, in his very first race, back in 1912. See pages 42 to 45.

Miss BEATRICE SHILLING 490cc Norton 25 August 1934

Beatrice Shilling, a Manchester University MSc, arrived at the mid-week Brooklands meeting on 6 June 1934. After three practice laps on her self-prepared 490cc Norton, she came sixth in her first race and third in her second, lapping at over 90mph. In a race report, 'The Motor Cycle' added the comment that "she had even made the pattern for casting the aluminium silencer fishtail, then finishing the casting to shape!"

In the picture on page 239 of the line-up for the August 1934 all-comers handicap race, she can be seen sitting quietly on her Norton, the third machine from the left, alongside Mortimer's big Brough, the eventual winner. In the three lap race she was to distinguish herself by lapping the Norton at 101.02mph, so winning her Gold Star. In a later race at the same meeting, she was re-handicapped by the timekeepers, finding herself on scratch and thus the first woman in a handicap race at Brooklands to give all her male opponents a start. She celebrated this by lapping at 101.85 mph, but was unplaced.

The supercharged version of the Norton as devised by Beatrice Shilling is seen here on its first appearance in June 1939. The centrifugal blower was designed to feed air into the petrol tank, now serving as a compressed air reservoir. Ridden by her husband, George Naylor, the blown Norton was disappointingly slow and there was little time for further development as the next meeting on 15 July that year was to be the last before the outbreak of war.

Sitting behind the uncomfortable-looking new petrol tank, the six foot tall Naylor could reach the handlebars. Beatrice Shilling, at five foot two inches, could not.

E C FERNIHOUGH   172cc Excelsior-JAP   25 August 1934

Eric Fernihough passes Charles Mortimer's 250cc TT Replica New Imperial during the same meeting in August 1934 as on the previous page. Fernihough on his little 172cc Excelsior-JAP was going really well, here lapping his friend, not for the first time in the race, now with a broad smile on his face as he sees the deflating rear tyre on Mortimer's machine.

Winning the 37 lap race at the extraordinary speed for such a small engine of 82.18mph, Fernihough was demonstrating yet again his mastery of tuning motorcycles so as to go as quickly as possible, as well as riding them skilfully and bravely.

His record breaking feats in particularly with both blown and unblown Brough Superiors tend to lead one to overlook the fact that his racing career began back in 1923 when, as a member of the Cambridge University MCC, he had given the boys on their ohv 350s a run for their money on his old sv 250cc New Imperial.

Few men did so much to uphold British prestige in the field of motorcycle engineering in the 1930s, specialising in what he saw as the 'Blue Riband' records, the standing-start and flying-start kilometre, and the classic one hour.

Nevertheless, his race lap records also added up, such as the s/s and f/s speeds of 104.63 and 123.59mph on his unblown Brough in 1935. The following year, in Germany, he took the blown machine to 98.91mph for the s/s kilometre and, later in Hungary, with a sidecar, to a new world's s/s kilometre at 80.49mph. Again in Hungary, in April 1937, his new solo and sidecar f/s kilometre records with the blown Brough were 169.80 and 137.10mph respectively.

Finally, at the combined car and motorcycle meeting at Brooklands on 3 March 1938, he was timed over the f/s kilometre at 143.30mph, the fastest speed ever by a motorcycle at the track.

Coming down to more mundane matters, Fernihough had from the outset dealt with the practical side of motorcycle racing – how to pay for it. Apart from the race and record bonuses paid by tyre, oil and fuel companies amongst others, tuning other competitors' machines at his Brooklands rented lock-up was a steady earner.

Finally, he came up with the bright idea of acquiring Bill Lacey's record-breaking Grindlay Peerless when, in 1930, Lacey moved to Nortons. Fernihough fitted the machine with a speedway JAP engine and hired it out, for £5 a time, so that aspirants for BMCRC Gold Stars could have, on it, a better chance of success.

C K MORTIMER   490cc Norton   27 July 1935

Amongst the few traditional annual events for motorcycles in the thirties were the Senior and Junior Mountain championships to decide who was that year's champion in each class.

The twenty-five lap races took place on what was known as the Mountain circuit, a new 1.1 mile long course commencing from the start line on the finishing straight, around the Members' Banking, down past the motorcycle pits, round the hairpin at the Fork and back up over the start and finishing line.

In the Senior race on 27 July 1935 Charles Mortimer had entered his Norton without great hopes because he had been told that it tended to be "a sort of medium distance tear-up" Many of the top riders were entered as well.

In the event it proved to be exactly as described, with much pushing and shoving, frames and exhaust pipes grounding and "bits of bicycle flying everywhere". To his complete surprise, at half distance, Mortimer found himself in the lead, which he managed to hold, winning the race at 70.43mph and being given what was to become his permanent nickname,'Champ'.

In the picture, behind the oil-stained Mortimer is Jock West, in the dark shirt. He was described by Joseph Bayley as "specialising in finishing second in the Hutchinson Hundred races: in 1935 and 1936 on a 498cc Triumph, at 96.90 and 100.01mph, and in 1937 and 1938, on a 346cc AJS, at 95.05and 92.48mph". The Triumphs were prepared by L W E Hartley.

C B BICKELL   499cc Ariel sidecar   14 September 1935

We have already seen that 'The Motor Cycle' trophy for the first multi-cylinder 500cc motor cycle to cover 100 miles in one hour was won by New Imperial in September 1934.

What was left out of the story on page 236 was the idea behind the award. As much as anything else, the publishers were concerned about the apparent determination of the British motorcycle industry to stick to the well-tried 'single' in the face of developments abroad. What was recalled in our story was that, as well as New Imperial, the Bickell brothers had also viewed the challenge with interest.

In 1931, Ariel Motors had introduced a new version of their revolutionary Square Four machine, with a 596cc engine. This still had four cylinders in a square formation, with two crankshafts geared together and a chain-driven overhead camshaft. The new engine worked as smoothly as did its parent, but giving more torque as well as rapid acceleration.

This new engine had caught the eye of the Bickell brothers who were nothing if not original. Before long, however, they knew full well that to make this engine reliable for long distance work at Brooklands was a well-nigh impossible task, especially as they had added a supercharger. The wide variations in cylinder temperature of the linered-down 600cc engine was bringing about blown gaskets and leaking head joints with monotonous regularity, whilst the cylinder base flange always threatened to part company with the crankcase.

But the Bickells always got, and gave, a great deal of pleasure out of racing their blown 499cc four cylinder outfit, and, over the s/s half mile, as here at the Brighton Speed Trials in 1935, the Ariel looked and sounded magnificent. Ben Bickell is seen in full flight, taking second place to Fernihough's Brough outfit at 68.70mph.

H R NASH   123cc New Imperial   28 September 1935

Riders line up for the start of the first all-comers three lap handicap race in the Hutchinson Hundred race meeting on 28 September. In the foreground, clutch lever depressed, H R Nash, on his faired-in 123cc New Imperial, is about to get away as the Chief Starter, 'Ebby' Ebblewhite drops his flag.

Nash had the New Imperial agency in Dorking, Surrey. He supplied not only road machines but also other models which could be modified for racing which he encouraged by example. New Imperial had reacted to the then current price-cutting war by producing the little 150cc 'Unit Minor' overhead valve model to sell at a record low price of seventeen guineas (£17.85).

As the new machine seemed to offer some sporting potential, Nash sold one to Charles Mortimer, but took it back in when, at first sight, it seemed a lost cause in racing terms. Not put off, Nash spent further time on the engine to the effect that Mortimer went on to win two races on it at Brooklands.

Further encouraged, Nash linered a 'Unit Minor' engine down to 123cc and, with the streamlining seen in the photograph in place, he took the machine to Belgium and secured new world standing and flying start kilometre and mile records at speeds over 80mph.

The financial crash of 1930 had immediate and far reaching effects in Great Britain, which even motorcycle racing at Brooklands could not avoid. The trade stopped bonus payments for racing and record breaking successes and, after 1930, the classic 200 mile races were discontinued, the Hutchinson Hundred remaining as the only long distance race on the calendar. Gradually the engineer/riders and team managers of the 1920s were being replaced by formally trained men such as the Bickell brothers, and Nash, most of whom ran their own businesses.

In many ways, Brooklands was undergoing changes as the decade passed, especially as the emphasis moved from the traditional outer circuit to the more artificial road racing format.

BMCRC Cup Day Meeting   23 May 1936

This photograph well illustrates the design of sidecars in the later years at Brooklands. Now the passengers were lying prone, with head to the rear, in what had become known as 'coffin' sidecars, invariably travelling with negligible comfort in the interests of weight saving.

Two first-hand anecdotes memorably illuminate this somewhat masochistic form of motorcycle racing at the track. The first was recalled by Charles Mortimer: "One incident was in the 1934 Hutchinson Hundred, in which I was on the little 150cc 'Grand Prix' New Imperial. Halfway through the race – I was lapping around the 85mph mark - I was passed by Les Archer's Velocette outfit.

"They came past quite slowly and immediately they were ahead of me I found myself gazing into the face of his passenger, Offord, who was, of course, lying down and facing rearwards. Slowly and deliberately Offord raised his hand to his nose and extended a thumb and four fingers. Whereupon, at that very moment, his sidecar wheel detached itself from its spindle and bowled merrily away into the undergrowth. Offord's face was a study as he covered his face and gently tapped Les on the behind with the other hand."

Mortimer went on to add that there was no real danger because the sidecars were by then fitted with a skid to guard against this eventuality. But pulling up safely was still hairy.

J S Worters, too, recalled one of his early 200 mile sidecar races when, on reaching the pits to refuel, his passenger leapt out of the sidecar, said "that's enough of that!" and disappeared into the crowd. Luckily, one of Worters' own pit crew was able to take over at once.

The Senior Brooklands Road Championship Race   17 July 1937

This rather long-winded race title celebrated the opening of the 2 miles, 470 yards Campbell road course soon after work was completed on the new concrete track extension laid down on the Brooklands infield in early 1937.

The photograph shows the altered face of the Members' Hill, the new 'Motor' pedestrian bridge spanning the new track, whilst the Home Banking, often known as the Members' Banking, still forms the familiar background.

The riders seen here are already spread out in the ten lap senior race: there was also a junior race in the day's programme. No 20, the fifth machine in the group, is Les Archer on a works 495cc TT Velocette, who, after a slow start, came through the field to come second to Harold Daniell's winning 490cc Norton. Daniell had also won the junior race on a 348cc Norton.

E C FERNIHOUGH   996cc Brough Superior-JAP   12 March 1938

With generous help from George Brough, Eric Fernihough had built two Brough Superiors with records in mind. The first, which was unblown, appeared in 1935 with a big-twin engine he had built from JAP parts installed in a 1927 frame with Webb front forks.

The engine, with its forward facing exhaust ports and two carburettors, was similar to the Joseph Bayley 1929 970cc Ariel-Anzani that Fernihough had seen and admired at the Brighton Speed Trials in 1934.

For 1936 he had prepared the blown machine, having a similar engine, again in a 1927 frame.

This version had been modified by the addition of dated bottom-link Harley-Davidson front forks which Fernihough disliked and only used because Brough fitted them to his standard machines. Henry Laird of Morgan fame supplied the supercharger and its installation was in the capable hands of Granville Grenfell.

It was on this second machine that Fernihough attacked the Brooklands flying kilometre record on 12 March 1938. He is seen in the picture setting off on one of his runs which finally set a new speed of 143.39mph, a figure which would remain unbroken.

E C FERNIHOUGH   996cc Brough Superior-JAP   23 April 1938

As we have already seen, Fernihough had set out to attack the Brooklands flying kilometre record on 12 March on his supercharged Brough Superior and, after several attempts, had been successful with one run at 143.39mph.

He now felt it was time for a pitch at the Class E outright flying start kilometre record held by Ernst Henne on a BMW. The German had set out on the kilo record trail in 1932, with a speed of 157.86mph. Always with BMW, Henne had improved on his own record virtually year on year since then until, in April 1937, Fernihough had halted that run with a new record at 169.85mph,

although the improvement was marginal, only 0.77mph. Inevitably Henne had responded with 173.67mph; but now Fernihough was ready.

Seen here, at Brooklands in March 1938, the Brough was now fully faired-in save for the front wheel. Early the following month, Fernihough and his team set out for Hungary.

After a number of shake-out trial runs, the first attempt on the record was made on the twenty third of April, when, at an estimated approach speed of 180mph, a gust of wind moved his machine slightly off course, causing the crash which was to cost Eric Fernihough his life.

Postscript from the notes of Dr Joseph Bayley

Fernihough's death was to pose the question: what had become of his unblown Brough Superior. In December 1938 it was taken over by a consortium including Brough, Beart, Pope and Rowland, Fernihough's friend and helper, who announced their intention to carry on his quest for the World's Record, using as a basis his surviving machine. In the brief period of time remaining before war was declared, nothing further had been heard of their plans.

Pope preferred to ride his ex-Baragwanath supercharged Brough that he had raced since 1934, now with recently fitted new Harley-Davidson/Castle front forks. So Beart meticulously rebuilt the surviving Fernihough engine, replacing both cylinder barrels as these showed signs of

porosity, and making new blower pipes to fit the rear facing inlet ports. The now supercharged engine was easily installed in Pope's frame.

Probably both Fernihough frames returned to Nottingham, without engines, gearboxes and fuel tanks; these now were the property of Mrs Fernihough. The remains of the supercharged machine on which he lost his life lay under covers in a corner of the factory in 1940. The engineless frame of the unblown machine no longer posed a question.

All rather a complicated answer to a simple question, but one which may throw some light on why no ex-Fernihough racing Brough Superior exists today.

D A Loveday 497cc Ariel 3 September 1938

Denis Loveday was one of the many genuine 'clubmen' riders at Brooklands, men who managed to hold down a full-time job whilst regularly competing at the track, usually with minimal trade support.

Now aged 93, the sprightly Londoner is today living happily in rural surroundings in Somerset, where, in 2006, the author caught up with him to record some of his Brooklands memories.

Apprenticed as a toolmaker, his first "proper" bike was a 1932 Blue Star BSA which his father got for him at trade price, £45, through a friend at BSA. Loveday used it daily until breaking his leg in two places riding it at a grass track meeting.

Back in action much later, he traded the BSA in for a dealer's £60 "banged about" 1932 KTT Velocette with a racing background which he got to run on petrol-benzole, then using it, still unregistered, to ride to and from work.

In 1933 he fancied trying it out at Brooklands. "You could buy the 'Motor Cycle' for thruppence and cut out a coupon to get you into the track for a shilling. If you were in an ACU club you could enter a race for five bob." Joining the BMCRC, he entered a three lap Round the Mountain race, finding his three-speed gearbox to be a handicap against the works Velocettes and Ariels with four speeds. However a 12:1 piston and a fifty/fifty "posh" mixture of benzole and aviation fuel, gave him a flying kilometre speed of 98mph, and with it, he began to enjoy some success.

He was now racing regularly, on Wednesdays and Saturdays. "We were only allowed to use the track on those days, starting at 2 pm because of early closing. No racing on Sundays, of course, because of Lord's Day Observance."

By 1936, as a qualified toolmaker he was earning 15/6d (77½ p) for a 47½ hour week. "I had a sponsor at that time. My father said I had to give Mother ten shillings on Saturdays. But when I opened my lunch box on Mondays there was ten bob in there as well. Later on my wife helped me out as she made more than me."

That year, Loveday won his 100mph lap Gold Star on a friend's 497cc Ariel Red Hunter, then was lent a similar machine by the Ariel works on which he continued to race until the end of 1939. He is seen in the picture (2), in a three lap outer circuit handicap in September 1938. Number 10 is Fullam's 499cc Vincent-HRD and, inside the ten foot line, his good friend and all too regular opponent, Bert Perryman on his 248cc Excelsior. Both men were to be entered in the last race the following year, described on page 268.

After that, in Loveday's own words, "somebody started a blooming war!"

A C PERRYMAN   248cc Excelsior   8 October 1938

Bert Perryman was a motorcycle clubman through and through, emerging onto the Brooklands scene in 1934 from his days in 'mud-plugging' and minor sprints, to take his place amonst the young, semi-professional riders in the road racing period at Brooklands.

Competing on a 248cc Excelsior and later on works-supported Ariels, his name appeared regularly in the race reports in the Isle of Man and in sprint events at Brighton and Gatwick as well as at Brooklands, especially with the advent of the new road racing extensions there.

Perhaps one of his most satisfactory days -despite the awful weather - came in October 1938, best described in his own words from his book A Clubman at Brooklands; "After the Gatwick meeting in June and Brighton in July, my last meeting of the year was at Brooklands, for a five lap race and ten lap Mountain race. I was unplaced in the first, but in the ten-lapper, the last of the that season and my last race on the Excelsior, I had a fine scrap with my old pal McDonnell on his Bickell-JAP. We were both limit men and had a two minutes, two seconds start on the scratch man, Ron Harris on a bored-out 502cc Norton. I realised that, at last, despite my fourteen and a half stone, I had a favourable handicap, and with a bit of luck could annex this race. I was No16 and Mac No17, and after I had shaken him off, not further challenged, I romped home the winner.

"This was the only Brooklands race I ever won with the Excelsior and a fitting finale to the '38 season, especially as it also clinched for me the BARC Aggregate Cup. So my Excelsior finished in a blaze of glory and I sold it to Norman Cox, the owner of the Sluggish Norton.

"I had enjoyed a trouble-free season with it, although it wasn't as fast as the best 250s. In fairness to it, I was always on benzole, a bit of a disadvantage round the Mountain when against the alcohol motors."

I B WICKSTEED   496cc Triumph   8 October 1938

Ivan Wicksteed's interest in motor cycles dated from his late schooldays, when he borrowed a friend's 1925 sv 250cc BSA to try his hand in the 1931 Schoolboys' Trial. Encouraged by winning a bronze medal for his efforts, he invested ten shillings - the equivalent to 50p – in a belt-drive, two-stroke Radco from his local scrapyard.

A machine clearly unsuitable for trials – the belt kept breaking – he managed to part exchange the Radco for a 500cc Norton, finally moving up to a 350cc Cotton-Blackburne on which he gained experience in scrambles. The potential of his latest machine tempted him to look in the direction of Brooklands, and making his first appearance at the track in 1934.

During his early attempts at the flying kilometre the Cotton finally registered 76.61mph, which Wicksteed felt was encouraging but inadequate, swapping the Cotton for a Rudge into which he fitted an ohv JAP engine.

Gaining experience at Brooklands all the time, in 1936 he was able to claim the much-coveted Gold Star with a lap of 101.64mph on his latest acquisition, a 500cc Excelsior.

Switching to Triumphs, he surprised everyone in 1937 by raising the fastest 500cc lap that year to 110.68mph. Still in search of more speed, he acquired one of the new Speed Twin Triumphs, which, after many setbacks, began to show serious promise, finally lapping at 107mph.

The offer of an Arnott supercharger could not be resisted, bringing more problems, not least the conflicting advice from those who ran blown machines. But with each improvement in power output, so the handling would deteriorate in direct proportion to the increase in speed.

Undeterred as ever, Wicksteed and his team made steady progress until the Triumph was lapping at 122mph, with a top speed of 127mph. They now felt that D C Minett's 500cc lap record of 116.63mph dating from April 1938 could be within reach and arrangements were made to make the attempt during the Hutchinson Hundred meeting on 8 October that same year.

The day dawned wet and with a strong south-westerly wind. However, as this was to be the last opportunity of the year, Wicksteed decided to go ahead. Despite the appalling conditions, his determination was rewarded with a new 500cc lap record of 118.02mph, a record which would never be beaten, as the track would be closed the following year, never to reopen.

N POPE 996cc Brough Superior-JAP 5 July 1939

Noel Pope was possibly one of the most competitive of all racing motorcyclists, his career dating from his debut at Brooklands in 1933. Apart from his track racing record, he had many successes in the Isle of Man and on circuits all round Europe both before and after the war.

However it is safe to say that his urge to break speed records on both two and three wheels is the side of Noel Pope that is most relevant to a book such as this. We have now reached the final years of the Brooklands story and it was in the late 1930s that the names of Fernihough and Pope both came into sharpest focus.

Whilst Fernihough was concentrating on his battle with the German record breaker Ernst Henne, wresting from each other the Class E World's flying start kilometre record, Pope had his eye on the Brooklands outright lap record which had stood to Fernihough at 123.58mph since 1935.

Early trials in 1939 on his favourite Brough, the ex-Baragwanath supercharged machine, now fitted with Harley-Davidson/Castle front forks, were inconclusive. Yet he still planned to attack the lap record, which he did during a clubman's day in April that year. But damp patches on the track put paid to his ambition.

Whilst in the Isle of Man in June 1939, he received his call-up – he was a reservist in the Tank Corps. Without delay, he was able to have Francis Beart rebuild the engine from Fernihough's unblown Brough which George Brough and Pope had taken over in December 1938. Fitted with the supercharger, the engine was installed in Pope's frame and all made ready for a final pitch at the lap record.

The first attempt on 24 June came to nothing due to the front piston tightening up. The last opportunity came on 5 July, when conditions were good enough for Pope to wring a lap out of the Brough at 124.51mph, thus beating Fernihough's six year old record by just under one mile an hour, and going into history as the fastest ever lap by a motorcycle at Brooklands.

BMCRC Mountain Championship Day   15 July 1939

It was, no doubt, with an inevitable sense of foreboding that the final meetings, both for motorcycles and cars, took place at Brooklands during the last weeks that the track remained open. In this paddock scene before the last ever motorcycle event on 15 July 1939, Francis Beart, on the right in the cap, is giving instructions to his rider, Johnny Lockett. The field had already been somewhat denuded by a number riders being called up for military service.

In the 25 lap race, Lockett on Beart's oversize 502cc Norton would prove to be an easy winner. In what would be a anticlimatic end to the twenty eight year history of motorcycle racing at Brooklands, Lockett was to lap the second place man two laps before the end of the race.

Lockett, along with Jock West, was one of the two riders who most impressed the very young Anthony Bayley at Brands Hatch after the war. (See Preface, page 8)

Postscript: Herbert Le Vack 1887 - 1931

For the men pictured on the previous page awaiting the start of the last motorcycle race at Brooklands, the imminent war might have seemed a good enough reason for racing being stopped, at least for the time being.

What no-one could have foreseen was that Brooklands would never reopen, at least for use as a race track. Leased to the War Department 'for the duration', a combination of major works carried out by Vickers to meet aircraft production requirements and extensive damage from air raids, left Brooklands by the end of the war in a parlous state. In view of this, 1946 saw the entire site sold to Vickers.

However this story of Brooklands should end on a more positive note. And there can be no better way than taking another look at the outstanding exponent of motorcycle racing in the history of the track. Here in the photograph, having just won a 1000cc race on his Zenith-JAP in 1922, is Herbert Le Vack, a picture of calmness, a man content with a job well done.

Le Vack was first employed in 1912 by Osbourne de Lissa, the British agent for the Swiss company, Motosacoche. Although having no formal engineering qualifications, Le Vack was already showing his brilliance as a motorcycle engine designer.

After the 1914-18 war he rode at Brooklands for the American Indian team until 1922, then joined J A Prestwick as chief designer in their racing engine department, where his name was to become law. Three years later, the company withdrew from racing, Le Vack then moving to New Hudson in a similar capacity until 1928, when he rejoined Motosacoche, his first employer, this time at their Geneva works.

Le Vack's career served as a showcase of his skills both as an engineer/designer and tuner. He laid down the pattern of most of the engines he used, prepared and developed them for racing and record breaking and eventually designed his employers' machines in their entirety.

His ability as a track rider was also second to none. He was the first to lap Brooklands at over 100mph and the first to do so on a 500cc machine. He won the only 500 mile race and six 200 mile races. He held the world's flying start kilometre and mile records in all five solo classes and in all three sidecar classes, a feat unique in the history of motorcycle record breaking.

Little is known about Herbert Le Vack the man. It has been said that he spoke quietly and little and did not make friends easily. He was not a 'clubbable' man. Highly regarded by the Brooklands motorcycle fraternity, he used his business skills to secure better bonus and retainer deals for many riders.

He is known to have been a family man. It is ironic that he was to die, aged 44, in a trivial road accident near Geneva, testing a new Motosacoche.

In his 1968 book The Vintage Years at Brooklands, Joseph Bayley wrote: "In my opinion, Le Vack was the greatest of all racing motorcylists. We shall not see his like again."